Resolving the Money Riddle.

How I Went From Sweet FA to $10 Million a Year in 18 Months.

Quantum Orange Pty Ltd

ISBN 978-0-6455480-0-6

First published 2008

Copyright 2008 - 2022 Paul Blackburn and Quantum Orange

quantumorange.com

Dedication

To all of you out there who have ever had the guts and determination to 'have a go' in the magical world and to all of you who have ever thought about it – this work is dedicated to shortening the distance between concept and cash in the bank. May your efforts be blessed.

If you don't already, you'll one day understand that your business has not just taught you lessons unable to be learned elsewhere, but also concepts you value more than the cash. I wish you well on your amazing and beautiful journey.

Fifty million reasons…

I used Paul's coaching services for our 350 staff during the growth of my business from $20 million to $50 million. After the business was sold he was the obvious choice as my personal coach. Ten years after we first met, Paul still stops me in my tracks with his insights and wisdom. With the start of our new business, we have taken out a huge insurance policy by using Paul's services as coach to our key people. I laugh all the way to the bank when I think about Paul's contribution to my wealth, health and, most importantly, my happiness.

Bob Kent

20 years and still going strong…

I've known Paul for close to 20 years now, since turning up in one of his early courses. In one 20-minute exercise he took me from failing my high school exams to distinctions at university. In another 4-hour exercise he taught me a skill that has since resulted in earnings of over $1 million. I have lost count of the number of people I have referred to the Beyond Success team and never once have they failed to deliver. Paul himself has had the courage, perception and insight to keep me learning from him, sometimes despite my best efforts to the contrary. I hold Paul and his legendary teaching ability in the highest regard.

Andrew Grant

A tidal wave…

Your Mental Toolbox workshop has really set my husband and I on the right path. Doing the course as a couple was beneficial while setting up our new business, Niche Partners, as we have been able to concentrate on each other's strengths. It seems that incredible opportunities are seeking us out and recently we've experienced some amazing coincidences – almost like positive omens – that have filled gaps that existed for years. I feel as though I am surfing on the top of a tidal wave, but now I trust that I will not wipe out, but will coast into shore. Thanks for inspiring us.

Janet Beckers

He's overqualified...
Paul's incredible understanding of the world, people and human nature makes him the ultimate life coach. I was amazed at how such profound ideas could be taught in a fun, powerful and simple way. He really opened my eyes and raised my awareness of peak performance and happiness in all areas of my life. I'm a devoted fan!

Steve Mason

Massive knowledge gain...
I would like to take the opportunity to thank you for an amazing weekend. As a master practitioner of NLP and personal coach, I knew some of the information you were teaching. However, it never ceases to amaze me how much more there is to know and learn. I loved the fact that the seminar was extremely useful for all walks of life and we were able to implement these techniques into our lives immediately. You have just given me even more inspiration to keep moving forward on my journey.

Angelina Zimmerman

Earthy and real...
Thanks for the mind-blowing workshop. Nice to see a born-and-bred Australian is such a rich source of solid, tested and proven motivational and personal development material.

David Guest

Fixed my money stuff...
Even though I knew I had financial beliefs that stank, and I sort of knew what they were, over the course of the weekend workshop, I understood them clearly for the first time. Removing them so quickly and easily has been a delight.

George Juross

Contents

CHAPTER 1
Understand it's not about the money 5

CHAPTER 2
Believe it's possible 29

CHAPTER 3
Dump your emotional baggage 51

CHAPTER 4
Face your fears 73

CHAPTER 5
Think abundance 99

CHAPTER 6
Surround yourself with success 117

CHAPTER 7
Leverage yourself 135

CHAPTER 8
Find your niche 159

CHAPTER 9
Stretch your prices 185

CHAPTER 10
Work on the business, not in it 203

CONCLUSION 223

REFERENCES 227

BIBLIOGRAPHY 231

INTRODUCTION

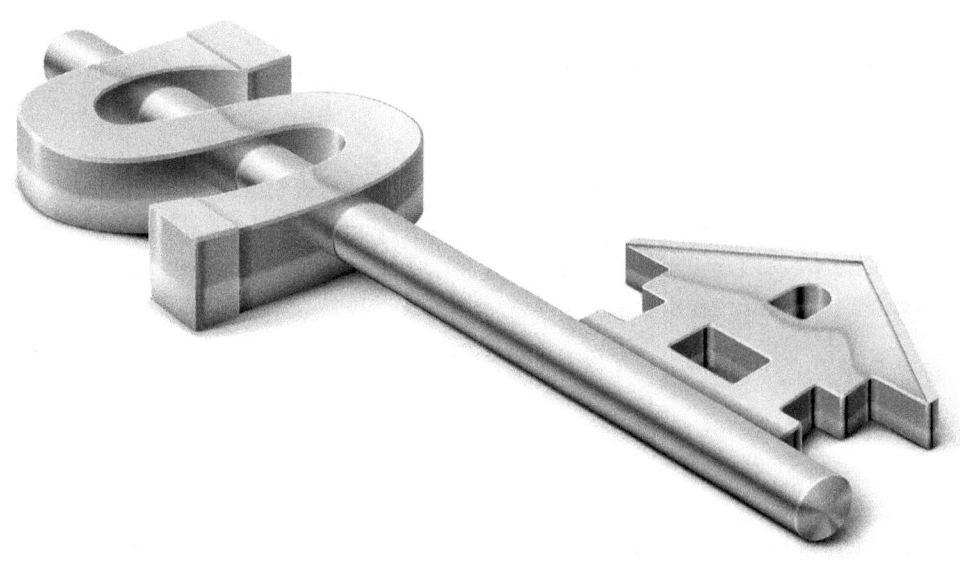

RESOLVING THE MONEY RIDDLE ▶ ▶ ▶

My wife Mary and I have been involved in the personal development industry in Australia for more than thirty years. It's a tough industry to crack. We sell intangible products that people only want to purchase when they've tried everything else.

During that thirty-year period we averaged about $350,000 a year gross turnover. And from that, we made $100,000 profit. In a good year it was $150,000. In the early eighties, that was great money. But earning the same level of income for 20 years running meant that at the end of that stint we were doing it a lot tougher than in the beginning. We were certainly feeling the pinch and beginning to wonder whether it would have been a smarter financial decision to remain schoolteachers. We knew ex-colleagues who had become high school principals with investment properties, superannuation and 12 weeks' holiday a year.

So, despite thirty years of experience behind us, we were still chasing customers. And we were tired of hearing people say "you've got world-class material. You could be world famous." We thought our material was great too but where were all the customers?

Then came the turning point. And this turning point is what this book is all about. Basically, our business grew from a $350,000 gross turnover cottage industry to a multi-million dollar success story. And it happened almost overnight.
Our success first came as a bit of a shock. Our products hadn't changed. My delivery hadn't changed. But all of a sudden, people were clamouring to buy from us.

From August 2006 to August 2007 we grossed $1.1 million. We tripled our business. Then the next month - September 2007 - we did again. We sold $1.1 million in that one month alone.

◄◄◄ INTRODUCTION

We were half way through the month before we realised what we were doing. We had been doing the things we'd always done - devoting ourselves to the delivery of the product and looking after people. Then halfway through the month Mary says to me, "Guess what? We could actually do as much in this month as we'd done all of last year."

And last year was more money than we'd earned in the previous 20 years put together.

At that point, we got a little bit excited. And a little bit nervous. But we watched as the business continued to grow.

And then in March 2008, our business pulled in $1.1 million (that magical number) again. This time, it was in an hour and a half.

The growth we were experiencing was a characteristic J-curve. I've seen similar results countless times when I've worked with people to help them get the breakthroughs in their businesses. Now it was happening to us. We were a classic case of the 20-year overnight success.

So how did I do it? What is the difference between my business two years ago and my business today? The difference is me. Each one of the chapters in this book will outline one factor that I think is vital for business – and personal transformation. Enjoy the ride.

CHAPTER 1
Understand it's not about the money.

CHAPTER 1 ▸▸▸

Before you begin reading this book, you need to ask yourself one question: "Should I go into business for myself?"

The average net income for the more than 15 million sole proprietorships in America is only $6,200 a year.

About 25 per cent of sole proprietorships do not make one cent of profit during a typical year.

It's even worse for partnerships. Forty-two per cent, on average, make no profits in a year. What about corporations? Only 55 per cent have any taxable income during a typical 12-month period.[1]

In Australia, the Productivity Commission estimates that up to 65,000 Australian businesses — that's 7.5 per cent of the total number of businesses — close their doors each year.[2]

> "About 25 per cent of sole proprietorships do not make one cent of profit during a typical year."

Does this scare you?

If it only emboldens you to take a chance, then read on.

The first step to becoming independently wealthy is to recognise that money doesn't matter, despite it probably being the motivator for most people wanting to go into business. While it may be a great ride getting rich, the most important lesson you can learn is to measure your success in terms other than monetary ones. Money magazine calls it "seeking something bigger than getting rich."[3]

◄◄◄ UNDERSTAND IT'S NOT ABOUT THE MONEY

While we all need money, and there are plenty of good uses for it, your focus needs to be on other measures of success. The need for challenge, excitement, creativity, personal satisfaction — whatever it is, you need to aim for more than just money.

Millionaires know this. That's why they are millionaires. They love what they do, and the money is just a bonus.

Let's get it straight up front. A focus on making money has kept me from generating the financial results I wanted.

> **"Your business is a personal development course on steroids."**

Why?

Money itself is not a big enough motivator when times get tough, as they inevitably must at some point. A fixation on the cash will stop you 'seeing' the breakthrough that would transform your business and your life.

For twenty years I have put the best part of 100 hours a week into making money. I've supported others, employed superstars, contributed first and asked to be paid later and generally been a good bloke — all to no avail as far as creating wealth was concerned.

What I failed to understand was something I was fond of telling everyone else.

Your business is a personal development course on steroids.

Like all self-help programs – you learn, 'get it' and transform or the lesson repeats and repeats and repeats.

CHAPTER 1 ▸▸▸

What is the lesson I was missing for 20 years?

If making money is your number one reason for going into business — get a McDonald's franchise.

What makes a millionaire tick?

In spending more than twenty years studying how people became wealthy, authors of *The Millionaire Next Door*, Thomas Stanley and William Danko discovered something very odd.

> **"Many people who live in expensive homes and drive luxury cars do not actually have much wealth."**

"Many people who live in expensive homes and drive luxury cars do not actually have much wealth," they recorded in their seminal book, *The Millionaire Next Door*. "Many people who have a great deal of wealth do not even live in upscale neighbourhoods."[4]

Can you imagine a millionaire settling for a $50 watch? Stanley and Danko couldn't, until they uncovered a startling statistic. For half of those surveyed, the most they'd ever spent on a wristwatch was $235. Ten per cent had never spent more than $47. Just one per cent of millionaires surveyed had shelled out $15,000 for a watch.

So, while Rolex advertises that its product is the ultimate sign of success in today's business world, the evidence doesn't stack up. In fact, the Rolex symbol "is a perfect way to jump start your career" — provided you are a high-powered lawyer, banker or stockbroker who needs to impress your clients! If you're interested in becoming a millionaire, then spend modestly and put the difference in the bank.

◂◂◂ UNDERSTAND IT'S NOT ABOUT THE MONEY

According to *The Millionaire Next Door*, affluent people typically follow a lifestyle advantageous to accumulating money. Stanley and Danko discovered seven common denominators among those who successfully build wealth:

1. They live well below their means.
2. They allocate their time, energy and money efficiently, in ways conducive to building wealth.
3. They believe that financial independence is more important than displaying high social status.
4. Their parents did not provide economic outpatient care (in other words, didn't financially support them once they were adults).
5. Their adult children are economically self-sufficient.
6. They are proficient in targeting market opportunities.
7. They chose the right occupation.[5]

Living a flashy lifestyle just isn't a priority for many of the world's billionaires. Until he gave away most of his money, Warren Buffett was the second wealthiest person on the planet. And yet he is content to drive a Cadillac. "They spend a lot of time giving away their money and their main goal in life is to solve big world problems, and that is why the car becomes less important," says Milton Pedraza, CEO of the Luxury Institute, a New York City-based research firm.

In contrast, people pursuing flashy lifestyles at the expense of financial independence are what one interviewee, a rancher from Texas, called "Big hat, no cattle." In other words: appearance of wealth at the expense of actual wealth.[6]

> "Are you 'big hat, no cattle'?"

CHAPTER 1 ▸▸▸

Numerous friends and acquaintances have told me over the years that investment properties are out of their league. "We just can't make the numbers work for us," they'll say, while they pull their expensive golf clubs out of their high-end SUVs, or while they polish the marble bench top in their newly installed kitchen. Thousands upon thousands of dollars spent on lifestyle, but they can't afford to take the drivers' seat when it comes to their assets.

Are you wealthy?

Best-selling financial author David Bach advises that, "before you can really start setting financial goals, you need to determine where you stand financially."

Here's a simple calculation to help you determine if you are wealthy:

- Multiply your age by your realised pre-tax annual household income from all sources of wealth except inheritances.

- Divide by ten.

- This, less any inherited wealth, is what your net worth should be.[7]

Are you close?

If you want to be a millionaire, your assets will need to exceed your liabilities by $1 million. Simple as that.

The next step is to spend less than you earn. Remember, wealth is not the same as income. Wealth is about what you accumulate, not what you spend. If you generate a good income each year, but it all goes on living high on the hog, you are not getting wealthier.

> "Instead of filling a vacuum, money makes one."

Don't become like Imelda Marcos and her shoes. The best pair is always the next pair — the only pair worth having. Don't buy into status objects or leading a status lifestyle. Once you're on the consumer goods treadmill, it's very hard to jump off, and all you're left with is a pile of depreciating assets. Hundreds of years ago, Benjamin Franklin warned us that "Money never made a man happy yet, nor will it. The more a man has, the more he wants. Instead of filling a vacuum, it makes one." And yet, we're still learning the lesson. So, learn your lesson today, and make your goal something greater than yourself. See it as your chance to contribute to the greater good, rather than simply funding a lavish lifestyle.

**Case study:
Look after the öre and kronor will look after themselves**

Ingvar Kamprad, the founder of IKEA, began his career as a money harvester by buying matches in bulk from a bazaar in Stockholm and selling them in his rural neighbourhood for a few extra öre per box. He was five years old. He soon graduated to Christmas decorations, ballpoint pens, seeds and fish, and by 17 years old he had started the small-scale retail business of IKEA.

CHAPTER 1 ▶▶▶

Today, IKEA carries about 9,500 products, employs more than 118,000 staff and, in 2007, generated $A32.6 billion from 522 million customers.

Despite his business success, it's widely reported that Kamprad drives a 15-year-old Volvo, flies economy class on budget airlines, and encourages IKEA employees to always write on both sides of a paper. Kamprad is sometimes spotted visiting IKEA for a cheap meal, and is known to buy Christmas paper and presents in the post-Christmas sales.

The joke in Sweden is that if Kamprad happens to drink an overpriced Coke from a hotel mini bar, he will go to a grocery store to buy a replacement. 1989, he told Forbes magazine that he was no longer as tight as he once had been, saying "I seldom wash disposable plastic glasses anymore."

This frugality is a principal part of the carefully managed image presented to IKEA employees and the general public. Kamprad knows his customers don't drive Bentleys or Rolls-Royces. And besides, as he says, "How the hell can I ask the people who work for me to travel cheaply if I am travelling in luxury?"

And watching his öre has enabled him to amass enough kronor to buy a villa in an upmarket part of Switzerland, a large country estate in Sweden and a vineyard in Provence. Not to mention the US$31 billion that Forbes magazine estimates he's now worth. In 2008, Forbes magazine named him the richest European-born person and the 7th richest person in the world.[8]

Passing the marshmallow test

In a famous study conducted at Stanford University in the 1960s, researcher Walter Mischel made the following proposal to four year olds: "If you wait until after I run an errand, you can have two marshmallows for a treat. If you can't wait until then, you can have only one — but you can have it right now!"

Some were able to wait as long as twenty minutes for the researcher to return, while others snatched the marshmallow within seconds of the researcher leaving the room.

> "Those who had resisted temptation were more socially competent as adolescents."

Twelve to fourteen years later, these children were tracked down and assessed. The differences between the two groups were dramatic. Those who had resisted temptation were more socially competent as adolescents. They were self-assertive, personally effective and better able to cope with the frustrations of life. They were less likely to go to pieces under stress, or become rattled under pressure; they embraced challenges and pursued them even through difficulties. They were self-reliant and confident, trustworthy and dependable. Most importantly, they were still able to delay gratification in favour of achieving their goals.

The children who had impulsively grabbed the marshmallow were found to be more troubled as adolescents. They were more likely to be stubborn and indecisive, to be easily upset by frustrations, to think of themselves as unworthy, to become immobilised by stress, to be mistrustful and resentful about not 'getting enough', to be prone to jealousy and envy, to overreact to irritations with a sharp temper. After all those years, they were still unable to delay gratification.

CHAPTER 1 ▸▸▸

If we were to look in on those kids now, who would be well and truly in their fifties, we'd find that some couldn't resist buying the latest model BMW, and those who had told themselves "If I go without now, I can have all the Ferraris I want and some to spare."

When Mary and I realised, for the first time, that we were going to make more than a million dollars in one month, we had to resist the temptation to crack open the champagne, buy an Aston Martin and book a long holiday in the sun.

> "If I go without now, I can have all the Ferraris I want and some to spare."

Instead, we chose to look at the situation simply from how much challenge and personal growth we could get from the experience. We chose to do what we'd always done and let the money sort itself out. In fact, it took quite some time for the money to flow through to us anyway. While we sold a lot of product that month, it didn't mean we had $1.1 million sitting in our bank account the next day.

When a business grows rapidly, you'll find yourself spending more than you are earning anyway. So, despite the influx of cash, we had the traditional problem we'd always had, which was that our outflow was greater than our inflow.

Why? As the money rolled in, it went out on venues that could hold larger crowds, printers for book runs, and wage costs for people to package our products and post them out. If we had sold $1.1 million in product the next month, the cash flow would have caught up. But, of course, we grew and so all the same problems were just expanded.

◀◀◀ UNDERSTAND IT'S NOT ABOUT THE MONEY

Mary and I were used to the problem of having more income and not being any better off. When we were both schoolteachers, we earned about $30,000 a year between us before tax. Like most people, we were spending more than we were earning, and we thought that an increase in income would solve that problem. So, we went into business for ourselves and were soon earning ten times our teachers' salaries. Ten times the money, ten times the income. Here we were, again, thirty years later, spending more than we were earning.

And then it dawned on me. Whether it's $30,000 a year, a month, or a minute, most of us are caught in a cycle of making money in order to fund our lifestyles. We needed to break that cycle.

> "Most of us are caught in a cycle of making money to fund our lifestyles."

The secret to breaking that cycle is simple: control your impulses. For most people, the gap between impulse and action is too small. This has certainly been my problem. In the past, having turned over a million dollars in a month, my impulse would be to splurge on an Aston Martin and justify it by saying 'why not?' My rationale would go: "I've just sold a million dollars at just one gig, and I only want to spend a third of it. I've got lots of these gigs booked over the next couple of years so why not spoil myself?"

You can see it's easy to justify anything if you want to. Whether it's a new flat-screen TV, a much-needed holiday, an extension on the house or a new one altogether, it's very easy to rationalise the expenditure, rather than invest in your future.

Most of us see the rewards for our hard work in material terms. "Once I've finished the end-of-year accounts, I'll buy myself a new dress," you might think

CHAPTER 1 ▶▶▶

to yourself, or say "When I get my bonus, I'm buying a new surround sound system". We trade our labour for money and then feel justified in rewarding ourselves for the effort. But imagine if you could retrain yourself so that there was a greater sense of reward in watching your bank balance grow?

If you could do that, you'd have jumped out of the rat race and no longer be looking for the big next thing you needed to buy. You'd gain your satisfaction elsewhere — from building something, from watching it grow, from planning for your future.

You may think that a bigger house is going to make your life better, spending that money on employing an offsider, investing in some new software, or buying some business books may help you to buy a dozen houses. But you would have to wait.

The trick is to place a pause between your impulse and actions. Your impulse is to buy the car (and by the way an airplane), but by taking time to pause between the impulse and the action, you'll see that your business needs the money more than you do.

> **"The trick is to place a pause between your impulse and actions."**

So, rather than blowing ten thousand dollars a month on payments for an Aston Martin, instead, I can feed that money into training people who can start producing more results. I'm taking the money that I would otherwise spend on toys and investing it in my future. In my case, training other people who can replicate what I do so that I can effectively be in several places at once. I realised that toys were merely temporary gratification.

Money is just a scorecard

Money needs to become nothing more than a scorecard. Money needs to be like a golf score. Without a score, you can't assess your performance and determine whether you played better today than yesterday. When you do keep score, you know that you're trying to do your best. You're not just whacking a little white ball around a golf course. Instead, you strive to become better each time you play. And if you're playing with a friend, you want them to go hard so that it can bring out the best out in you.

> "Money needs to become nothing more than a scorecard."

In the same way, keeping track of your money can provide you with a scorecard. And, like any worthwhile challenge, mastering money can help you reach your ideal potential. As Donald Trump says: "Money was never a big motivation for me, except as a way to keep score. The real excitement is playing the game."[9]

Gordon Gekko, Michael Douglas' character in the 1987 movie, Wall Street, is wrong when he says 'greed is good'. He tells stockholders of a struggling company that "Greed is right. Greed works. Greed clarifies and captures the essence of the evolutionary spirit. Greed in all of its forms — greed for life, for money, for love, knowledge — has marked the upward surge of mankind." At the end of the movie, we witness his downfall which reconfirms what we've known all along: greed is not good.

While unadulterated greed is destructive, so too is believing that money is the root of all evil. Instead, it is rampant 'love of money' that has been the cause of much human suffering.

CHAPTER 1 ▸▸▸

Money is merely a means of exchange — it is simply printed paper, or numbers on a screen. When I hold fifty dollars in my hand, it is nothing more than the representation of the time it took me to earn it. It is a symbol of all my effort, blood, sweat and tears, transformed into physical matter for me to barter with.

In my personal wealth seminars, I like to remind people of what happens when a population stops believing in its currency. Before World War II, for example, Germany was slumped in a depression and inflation went through the roof. From mid-1922 until mid-1923, prices increased by more than 100 times.

This rapid rise in inflation is well illustrated by the postage stamps that were issued during this period. In 1920 the highest valued stamp issued was for four marks. By 1923 the denominations were changing so rapidly that the post office could not design new stamps fast enough and resorted to using old dies and then overprinting them with new values. The highest value reached in 1923 was for 50 billion (50,000,000,000) marks.

> **"Money is merely a means of exchange - it is simply printed paper, or numbers on a screen."**

With prices doubling over the course of a day, wages were paid daily or several times a day, and the whole family would immediately spend the money before it lost value. *In The Black Obelisk*, a novel set in 1923, Erich Maria Remarque describes this practice:

> Workmen are given their pay twice a day now - in the morning and in the afternoon, with a recess of a half-hour each time so that they can rush out and buy things - for if they waited a few hours the value of their money would drop so far that their children would not get half enough food to feel satisfied.[10]

◄◄◄ UNDERSTAND IT'S NOT ABOUT THE MONEY

The currency depreciated because the German people stopped believing in its value. In other words, a fifty-dollar note is worth only as much as the value you place on it.

This is why people with lots of money can let it slip through their fingers like water. They place less value on it because so little of their own energy was required to produce it.

Can the person who charges $10,000 for a day's work really be worth that much more than the person who can command only $100? Of course not. The money we make is irrelevant when it comes to who we are. Income has nothing to do with good or bad, despite what many of us are taught.

And besides, if you live a comfortable, middle class life in the Western world, then guess what? You've already made it. If you have assets of more than $61,000, then you're in the top 10 per cent of the global wealth league table. To belong to the top one per cent of the world's wealthiest adults you would need more than $500,000, something that 37 million adults have achieved.[11]

Resolve the money riddle

One of the most important lessons to learn about money is that it should never change your values. After twenty years of studying millionaires across a wide spectrum of industries, Stanley and Danko concluded that "the character of the business owner is more important in predicting his level of wealth than the classification of his business."[12] Making money is only a report card. It allows you to monitor your success — it should never be more than that.

> **"The character of the business owner is more important in predicting his level of wealth than the classification of his business."**

CHAPTER 1 ▸▸▸

It is important to divorce yourself from the idea that financial wealth will make you a better person. You'll still be the same person with the same problems, only they'll be magnified by your money - hard to believe, when we're all taught that money will solve our problems. But if your marriage is not working, or your relationship with the kids isn't great, or you are dissatisfied with your career and you have gout, the only change you'll find is that you have more money to throw at the problem. It won't make the problem go away. You'll still be the same grumpy, gouty person you were before, but you'll be living in a bigger house and driving a fancier car.

Money remains a riddle in our lives that we never solve until we learn to separate ourselves from it. As long as you need money, the money owns you. And as long as the money owns you, then you'll act according to your internal scripting.

Most people in the Western world have all sorts of strange hang-ups about money. In fact, it's often easier to talk about sex than it is to talk about money. We are overburdened with scripting we learn from our culture about money. We learn that money doesn't grow on trees. Money is hard to come by. People with money aren't nice. Only crooks make lots of money.

> **"As long as you need money, the money owns you."**

If you were to sit down and write down a list of all the common clichés surrounding money, you'd rapidly find a full page. And while phrases like "money doesn't grow on trees" seems harmless enough, when they are hammered into our subconscious they become a program that is very hard to break away from.

From early childhood, we absorb the financial lessons around us. We watch our wage slave father slump exhausted in his chair, muttering 'another day, another dollar' under his breath. Or perhaps we see the money slip through his fingers as he laughs 'easy come, easy go'. Maybe we hear him scoffing at his financially successful friend who 'throws his money around and expects everyone to be impressed'. Or perhaps we watch him spend lots of time and energy competing with others and hating anyone else who achieves success.

> **"From early childhood, we absorb the financial lessons around us."**

We observe our mother overspending at the half yearly sales and then cutting up her credit card in disgust. Perhaps we watch her battle with her weight, meanwhile insisting we eat every morsel of food on our plates. Or we hear the next door neighbour complain about the latest drama with speeding fines, smash repairs and lost licences that is costing her a fortune. Whether there's plenty of money or not enough, we learn those lessons early and the subsequent internal programming means we repeat those same mistakes for the rest of our lives.

Let's look at an example. Say your parents struggled to put food on the table when you were small. They never said anything overtly, but as a child you recognised their pinched expressions and the slim pickings in the refrigerator. You'd hear your father saying "Just when we seem to be getting on top of things, something else goes wrong." What sort of impact would that have on you later on? Would you be able to see the financial opportunities as they were presented to you? If you could, would you be able to grasp them with both hands?

Probably not.

CHAPTER 1 ▸▸▸

Alternatively, if you grew up in a household where the predominant message about money was that people who make lots of money are not to be trusted, then it would be no surprise to grow up thinking that the man down the street with a nice house must have underworld connections or else be falsifying the accounts at work. How else could he have that much money?

Now, I'm not saying that everyone is legitimately making their money, but the vast majority of people are. But if my life script is that "people with money can't be trusted" then I will subconsciously search for evidence to prove my already established belief. I'll find lots of examples of people who lie, cheat and steal for a profit.

But imagine if you were able to dismantle that program? Imagine opening your eyes to all the independently wealthy people who give up their time for good causes?

> **"Examine the messages you tell yourself about money, and if you don't like them, change the CD!"**

It is easy to find evidence to prove your belief system about money. If you think the world is full of crooks, you'll get ripped off and it will reinforce your belief. If you believe the world is full of kind and helpful people, that's how you'll experience life.

To reprogram your life script about money, you need to examine your core beliefs and then take active steps to change the core beliefs that are not supporting you. It's as simple as examining the messages you tell yourself over and over about money, and then changing the CD!

Face your financial fears

We must learn to live without the emotional attachment to money. And you must learn to live without the physical need for it. To do this, there are two emotions to be mastered: the fear of loss and the greed to get.

When our children were small, Mary and I spent eighteen months living in a caravan with no running water and no electricity. After deciding to close shop in the city and head for the country, it was rather less idyllic than we'd hoped. Aside from cooking on an old stove and washing two little kids in a bucket, Mary's mother joined us too, so we had three adults and two kids cramped in an old caravan.

Now, I know that if I lost all our money and we had to live in a tent, Mary would come with me. And we'd have a great time. Sure, we'd complain about the lack of showers and the confined conditions, but I know — as does Mary — that we can be happy together anywhere.

> "The freedom to have a shot is fundamental to success."

The experience in the caravan taught us never to be afraid of being broke. We know that we'd be OK. Without that fear we are free to 'have a go'.

This is fundamental to success — the freedom to have a shot without being overly concerned about the negative consequences.

CHAPTER 1 ▸▸▸

People are afraid of being broke, and so are too conservative as a consequence. Extract yourself from the fear of loss and you free yourself to be daring.

The next thing to do is to remove the opposite — the greed to have money. While these seem to be diametrically opposed feelings, they are actually different versions of loss. Greed comes when we believe we won't get another chance. When we believe there aren't enough pieces of pie to go around. The bottom line feeling is lack, or a belief that there's not enough to go around.

There's obviously more wealth in the world now than there was 100 years ago, or ten years ago, or even last week. In fact, governments around the world are famous for setting up places called mints that will print money and share it around. While that might seem like an over-simplistic economic analysis, there is essentially a never-ending flow of the stuff.

> "Greed comes when we believe that there aren't enough pieces of pie to go around."

Most people ignore this and see the evidence of lack around them. They believe that hard work, or luck, or a bit of both, will make a fortune. And it's true that hard work and luck play their part — alongside belief that there's plenty out there for everyone. (In fact, relying on the recipe of hard work and good luck as the only two ingredients is the reason why most people are not wealthy. Join me at any gathering of a thousand people and I can probably find you 900 hard working, honest, reliable people who will never become independently wealthy.

Greed causes us to make poor judgements, because we make financial decisions based on our programming, rather than on logic and analysis. We need to find a balance between impulse, intuition and intellect. Instead, we run down the path of least resistance and follow our internal scripting.

◄◄◄ UNDERSTAND IT'S NOT ABOUT THE MONEY

Making the world go round

While I've spent this chapter outlining why money doesn't matter, there's one reason that it does: you can change the world for the better.

Since our business skyrocketed, Mary and I have been looking at what we want to do with our money. Like most people, there are some pretty obvious things: settle the mortgage, ensure our kids are financially secure, pay off the credit card debts.

But we're also dreaming and scheming with our two girls about the things we could do to change the world: orphanages in third world countries, scholarships for underprivileged children, seeding small businesses with great ideas. In reality, we don't need another house, boat, car, plane or hovercraft. Instead, we're thinking about how to spend our money in the best way possible so that the world benefits.

> "Spend the first half of your life earning a fortune and the second half of your life giving it away."

Of course, using your money for good is not a new idea: by 2007, two of the world's richest men, Bill Gates and Warren Buffet, had pooled more than $38 billion to reduce world poverty. The Rockefeller Foundation, established with money from that family's oil empire, is now considered one of the most influential charities in the world, and steel merchant Andrew Carnegie once famously said: "I'll spend the first half of my life earning a vast fortune and the second half of my life giving it away, while doing the least harm and the most good."[13]

CHAPTER 1 ▶▶▶

Things to think about…

- While it may be a great ride getting rich, seek out something bigger than just making money and accumulating assets. Ask yourself: what am I trying to achieve beyond becoming rich?

- Avoid pursuing a flashy lifestyle at the expense of financial independence. Remember: big hat, no cattle.

- Wealth is not the same as income, so spend less than you earn. How will you achieve this?

- Don't get caught in a cycle of making money to fund your flashy lifestyle. Break that cycle by controlling your impulses.

- Solve the money riddle by separating yourself from your financial success. Money is just a scorecard — it won't make you a better person, and it won't solve your problems.

- Reprogram your life script about money by examining your core financial beliefs. Ask yourself: what are my money programs? Listen to the messages you tell yourself, and then if you don't like them, change the CD!

- Face your financial fears. What is the worst that could possibly happen if you lost the lot?

- Use your money to make the world a better place. What will you do?

◀◀◀ UNDERSTAND IT'S NOT ABOUT THE MONEY

CHAPTER 2
Believe it's possible.

CHAPTER 2 ▸▸▸

"For those who believe, no proof is necessary. For those who don't believe, no proof is possible."

I'm fond of quoting this line in my workshops when people say "I can't" or "It won't work" or "It's impossible".

Success is as simple as that, really. Some people say "I can't" and others ask: "Why can't I?"

> **"Believe in the possibility of achieving your goal."**

I'm not saying spectacular success is as simple as believing in yourself. In fact, I don't think believing in yourself is actually a factor in success. There have been plenty of misguided souls who believed in themselves and, despite their lack of skills or aptitude, saw their businesses go bust and their dreams crumble. Time and tide wait for no man, and I'm not suggesting you take the King Canute approach (he commanded the tide to recede as he sat enthroned on the beach in England, getting increasingly wet).

The real message is: believe in the possibility of achieving your goal. Once you start to believe it's possible, that quite conceivably it could happen, then you can start thinking about what you need to do to make it happen.

Thomas Watson, the founder of IBM, (who famously speculated that "there is a world market for maybe five computers" in 1943) attributes the success of his company thus:

> IBM is what it is today for three special reasons. The first reason is that, at the very beginning, I had a very clear picture of what the company would look like when it was finally done. You might say I had a model in my mind of what it would look like when the dream — my vision – was in place.

The second reason was that once I had that picture, I then asked myself how a company which looked like that would have to act. I then created a picture of how IBM would act when it was finally done.

The third reason IBM has been so successful was that once I had a picture of how IBM would look when the dream was in place and how such a company would have to act, I then realised that, unless we began to act that way from the very beginning, we would never get there.

In other words, I realised that for IBM to become a great company it would have to act like a great company long before it every became one.[14]

So rather than saying your positive affirmations for fifty years and hoping that they'll become true, instead, believing it is possible is the first step on the long journey to success. Belief is the ignition switch that helps you to put the wheels in motion. Belief enables traction. Once you believe, and only then, can you ask yourself "if this is possible, what do I need to do?"

> "Belief is the ignition switch that helps you to put the wheels in motion."

In my case, for the best part of 10 years, I was surrounded by evidence that there was a heap of money in training people to be coaches. Yet, I always found some way to undermine the value of other people's successes. Sure there were people out there making millions, but maybe they weren't as honest as us. Maybe they had millions of dollars for marketing. Maybe they had a better location. The truth was, I just couldn't see the opportunity.

CHAPTER 2 ▸▸▸

> **"Are you swimming in a sea of possibilities?"**

In *Cracking the Millionaire Code*, Mark Hansen and Robert Allen describe a dramatic experiment in which researchers placed a large fish in the middle of an aquarium with minnows to feed on.

The fish fed to his heart's delight. Then, the researchers placed a glass partition in the tank, dividing it in two. After the pike had eaten all of the minnows on his side of the partition, he could see the other minnows through the glass but he couldn't get to them. He thrashed, he bumped, he bashed his body against the glass partition, but to no avail. He finally formed a belief that it was impossible for him to get to those fish. He stopped trying.

Then, the researchers removed the glass partition and allowed the minnows to swim all around him. He could smell them. He could see them. He could feel them. But he believed that those fish were no longer available to him – that they were forever locked away from him – that it was impossible for him to win. So he starved to death in the middle of an aquarium full of food.[15]

This was me — swimming in a sea of possibility, but unable to see the opportunities that were right before my eyes.

When I first started training coaches, I didn't believe anyone would want to train as a coach for a fee. Instead, I thought, "I'll have to train them and then see if I can earn some trailing commission from what they earn over the years and we'll end up recouping the costs of training eventually." Once that belief was established in my mind, the right people turned up to reflect that belief. Then, last September, somebody said to me "Why don't you price coaching training at $25,000 and just have a go?"

I knew I couldn't get $1,000 for it. I'd been in this game for 25 years and knew more about it than this Johnny-come-lately with the crazy ideas. But I went away and thought about it. And I asked myself: "Is it possible? What have I got to lose?"

And here's where the shift happens. I began to question myself: "Maybe I'm not right. Maybe this is possible." Once you start to believe in the possibility, then magic can happen. "Whatever the mind of man can conceive and believe, it can achieve. Thoughts are things!" says Napoleon Hill in *Think and Grow Rich*.

> **"Whatever the mind of man can conceive and believe, it can achieve."**

When I went to my next conference, I was fairly convinced I'd crash and burn, but during the process of presenting, I told the audience that anyone interested to learn how to do what I do — success coaching — was welcome to hang around at the end of the presentation. 20 people stayed, and six people purchased coach training on the spot — at $25,000 each.

That was enough to convince me that perhaps I had been wrong. Perhaps I could sell coach training.

Seven days later I got another chance, and this time sold more spots. And seven days later, on my third attempt, 23 people put their hands up and said: "I'm in".

So what changed? The audiences were similar. My talk was the same. The difference was me; I began to think "It's possible". And after that, "If it were to happen — what would I have to do?".

CHAPTER 2 ▸▸▸

The shift is from doing nothing (because we can't see it happening) to doing something. Specifically, doing whatever it is we have determined must be done in the light of it all being possible.

> "How do you open your eyes to the possibilities?"

In *Getting Everything You Can Out of All You've Got*, author Jay Abraham asks his readers if they recognise the following names: Frank Howser, Lewis Crandal, and Richard and Maurice McDonald.[16]

Apparently, two young guys once asked Frank Howser to design and construct a trade show booth for them. They couldn't pay him cash, but offered him stock in their start-up business. Frank said no; the two men were Steve Wozniak and Steven Jobs, and their small start-up company was Apple. Lewis Crandal sold his share in a store to his partner, Mr Woolworth, for $1,200. Richard and Maurice McDonald sold their name, alongside their hamburger stand to Ray Kroc, who went on to build a multibillion-dollar organisation.

These guys never saw the opportunities that were right in front of them.

So, how do you open your eyes to the possibilities? You need to change your paradigm — the way you make sense of the world in your head and define the boundaries of what can and cannot be achieved. Oscar Wilde said he could "believe anything provided it is incredible." Jay Abraham calls it "adopting a possibility-based mind-set that looks for new, different, and better ways to attain a goal or solution or address a situation."[17]

Change your paradigm and you change your world — new insights, knowledge and understandings open up. Our perception is affected first and foremost by whatever principles are at the centre of our lives. Perception in turn governs our elementary beliefs, attitudes and behaviours towards others and the world around us. So, perception reaffirms our principles and our principles reinforce our perception. It becomes a vicious or a virtuous circle — depending on whether the belief supports you or holds you back.

> **"Change your paradigm and you change your world."**

Think of the paradigm shifts in your own life. If you are married, recall what it was like to be single. What happened to your paradigm of life when you married? If you have children, remember how much your life changed when your first child arrived? You see an entirely new world. You look at life through a new paradigm resulting in fundamental, dramatic and revolutionary changes.

The world changes fast and many people, not to mention enterprises large and small, fail to see the next wave or see it and dismiss it. Our world is in a permanent state of flux, and even though you might miss one opportunity, it doesn't mean that there's not going to be another opportunity somewhere in some other niche for you.

New technology brings new innovators to our world. Fifty years ago we were impressed with supercomputers the size of warehouses. Today, we carry more powerful memory sticks around in our top pockets. The customers of the future are digital natives who cannot comprehend a life without remote control, have never heard the sound of a telephone dialling, and don't understand how anyone could have thought Pacman or Space Invaders was cool. In this world, the comments of Sir William Preece, Chief Engineer of the British Post Office,

CHAPTER 2 ▶▶▶

seem laughable. In 1876 Preece declared: "The Americans may have need of a telephone, but we do not. We have plenty of messenger boys."[18]

There are dozens and dozens of stories out there of people who didn't believe it was possible — everything from the four minute mile to man walking on the moon. But technological advancement is breaking paradigms faster than ever before. Here's a great little story about three Scottish businessmen who decided to publish three little volumes called Encyclopedia Brittanica in 1768. Their work, not surprisingly, emphasised the pressing concerns of the time. Curing of diseases in horses, for instance, covered 39 pages, while the reference for woman simply read 'the female of man'. The first edition even used careful calculations to estimate the number of species on Noah's Ark — 177 in total.

The idea of compiling knowledge blossomed and by the 1920s Britannica was purchased by Sears Roebuck and moved to Chicago, where American mass marketing drove the revenues sky high.

By 1990, however, CD ROMs were popular for their ability to pack lots of information into one portable and uploadable disk. Microsoft saw a possibility and purchased Funk and Wagnalls encyclopaedia, which they repackaged as Encarta. But those people at Brittanica were sure that people still wanted 24 volumes on their bookshelf.

> **"Technological advancement is breaking paradigms faster than ever before."**

By 2000, Britannica's revenues were in a downward spiral. And then, in 2001, a man called Jimmy Wales embarked on a collaborative experiment to catalogue the sum of human knowledge and provide it to the world for free. Wikipedia was the result.

Jimmy Wales is an inspiring example of someone who believed that something great was possible. He had a vision that, regardless of whether you lived in Boston or Botswana, you could access the same information and knowledge. By 2007, online encyclopaedias in 250 languages were gaining more than 1,700 articles a day, and by January 2008 the English Wikipedia alone had more than two million articles.

> **"Are you going to do it?"**

For most people, the idea of leaping out of a plane is not possible until they stand on the ledge looking out at the expanse of sky with nothing to save them but a parachute strapped to their backs. The possibility of skydiving has always been there — everyone knows someone who has done it. But it is only when we are faced with the question — "Are you going to do it?" — that we begin to imagine stepping off that platform.

So, there are only two easy steps to believing, and they are:

1. Embrace the idea that it could be possible; and then
2. Put some action behind the concept.

CHAPTER 2 ▶▶▶

Case study:
A hot idea

Hotmail co-founders Sabeer Bhatia and Jack Smith had wanted to start a company, and had been brainstorming possible business ideas for a few months. They wanted to email each other notes, but didn't want to risk their bosses accessing their email and discovering that they were spending their working hours on personal projects. The problem continued to frustrate them both until the light bulb went off: free email accounts that can be accessed anonymously, over the web.

In his book *The Nudist on the Late Shift,* Po Bronson says that "Any disgruntled employee who had ever worried about an employer reading his email could have had the idea before Jack and Sabeer. Anyone could have had the idea. You could have had the idea. I could have had the idea. In this new era of the Internet, to come up with a good idea you don't have to be an übergeek who understands fibre-optic switching and site mirroring and massively parallel processing. And the best ideas are right under your nose."[19]

Bhatia agrees, describing "two 27-year-old guys who had no experience with consumer products, who had never started a company, who had never managed anybody, who had no experience even in software. Jack and I were hardware engineers. All we had was the idea."

But what an idea. Soon, Bhatia and Smith were being rejected by venture capitalists across the country, eventually convincing Draper Fisher Jurvetson to finance their dream with $300,000 in exchange for 15 per cent of the company.

> The financial backers praised their idea, but wondered how they would attract members and build a company around it. Nevertheless, Bhatia and Smith got their seed capital and launched Hotmail on 4 July 1996 (American Independence Day), symbolising 'freedom' from ISP-based email and the ability for users to access their inbox from anywhere in the world.
>
> Just 30 months after its launch, Hotmail became the world's largest email service, with more than 30 million active members.
>
> To put this growth into perspective, it took Canada around 400 years to reach its current population of 31 million — a number that Hotmail had overtaken within three years. The Hotmail user-base grew faster than any media company in history — faster than CNN, faster than AOL, even faster than Seinfeld's audience.
>
> And Draper Fisher Jurvetson realised a tidy return on their $300,000 investment. Hotmail was sold to Microsoft in 1998 for a reported $400 million.

Setting yourself up for success

If you could find out a secret that would guarantee your success in everything you attempted, would you treat it like a valuable tool and commit yourself to using it, even if you did not understand how it could possibly work? If it was the silliest thing you ever heard of, but you knew that it worked well for others over extended periods of time, would you stick with it anyway?

CHAPTER 2 ▸▸▸

It sounds too simple to be true, but setting goals for yourself will make the road to success less rocky.

It's as easy as that. Goal setting helps you decide what you want, and exactly what you need to do to get there. Once you know what you need to do, you can start putting in the hard work required.

Also, setting your own goals helps you become more confident and motivated. The most motivated and confident people are those who know what they want, know how to get it, and know exactly what to do to maximise their chances of achievement.

> "Olympic athletes rate goal setting as the most effective strategy in enhancing performance."

Professional athletes have known this for years. In 2000, *The Sport Psychologist* magazine published the findings of a study, which found that "Olympic athletes rated goal setting as the most effective strategy in enhancing performance."[20] In an earlier study, the same researchers found that athletes from 18 different sports at four separate American universities who used goal-setting techniques performed more successfully than athletes who did not.[21] In another experiment, reported in a 1995 edition of the same magazine, 90 per cent of female basketball players who used goal setting increased their free throw percentage.[22]

If goal setting can improve free-throw performance, then what could it do to improve your business?

Time and again, sociological experiments have demonstrated that specific, challenging goals result in better performance than vague goals, no goals, or people simply trying to 'do their best'.

Putting things down in black and white is the key. There is a magic that mobilises the brain when we set a goal on paper. In simple physics (which has nothing to do with the magic) when you write down a goal, it makes its first step into the physical plane. Before this time, your goal has existed purely in the esoteric thought patterns that rattle around inside your head. Jean Houston, codirector of the Foundation for Mind Research, explains it this way: "The primary purpose of your brain is to do exactly what you tell it to do." [23] Consequently, writing down your goals is one of the most basic secrets of success, whether you like it or not.

If the secret to success is so simple, is there any reason why you shouldn't start doing it today?

> "The primary purpose of your brain is to do exactly what you tell it to do."

Speak success

You can't live an unlimited life if you're limiting yourself with your language. I have a client who can't start a sentence without sharing a problem. So, we live in a warm climate but the sun dries out our skin. Rather than reflecting on how wonderful it is to live in a sunny country, she's complaining about the cost of moisturiser.

"I know there's drought around the country, but does it have to rain when I want to play tennis?" she asks. Her friend scoops the pool in the lottery and now "all the hangers-on will be after her cash." If I pointed out her worldview, she'd say I was crazy. But I'm less so than her. She's just never listened carefully to her own language and examined what it translates into.

We need to take the time to literally listen to what we are saying. A personal trainer will tell you to keep a food diary if you want to lose weight. In the process of keeping that diary, you'd discover some shocking secrets about your

CHAPTER 2 ▸▸▸

eating habits; and you'd also have a roadmap for change. I suggest that each of us needs to use the same technique to keep a track of your words. Easier said than done, but a very powerful exercise to help you see what attitudes you need to change.

When we change our language, we produce a change in ourselves. Let me tell you something that we all know: 'it won't hurt' is a lie. As soon as these words are spoken, a sensation comes to mind — pain. Our brain immediately processes the word 'hurt' and begins to imagine all the needles, cuts, bruises and broken bones that we've had in our lives. The little word 'won't' is simply ignored by our brains.

If you are going to be successful, you need to speak success. That means altering your language so that success becomes a natural result of your attitude. When a bride walks down the aisle on her wedding day, she doesn't expect to get divorced. She's expecting that her marriage will be a success. She believes she can make the relationship work. Her attitude is "this can work". That attitude of expectation is, to me, the fundamental key in a relationship. As soon as we focus on, "we're having problems," then we stop looking for the skills that we need to make the thing work.

> **"You won't be successful if you speak the language of defeat."**

Whether it's marriage or business, the positive attitude required is the same. And language provides the key. We can't expect to be successful if we are speaking the language of defeat.

But actions speak louder than words

If you look at the difference between those who do and those who don't, it's all down to action.

When most people buy a 12-month gym membership, they have a vision of how that membership will transform their lives. They'll picture a healthier, slimmer, fitter and more attractive version of themselves walking around feeling fantastic about life. And then they only go for three weeks.

Why? They'll say "it's boring" or "I can't find the time". Well, that's true. It is boring and there are always other things that need to be done. There's probably not much that's more boring than sitting on a pushbike going nowhere.

If you look at the short-term outcome — you get hot and sweaty, feel uncomfortable and expend an hour that could be used doing other, more urgent tasks — sooner or later you're not going to the gym anymore.

> "Focus on the long-term benefits."

However, if you can keep focused on the long-term benefit, then you find yourself going to the gym more regularly. You find that you're no longer puffing when you walk up two flights of stairs. You discover you're tightening your belt a couple of notches and people are commenting on 'how well you look'. The effort will begin to pay off and the results will reinforce your behaviour.

I spoke to a fitness fanatic the other day and I asked what motivates him. He said "I have two grandmothers: one sat in her sedentary lifestyle, whinging and whining about getting old, and died aged 68. The other one is approaching 90 and still walks every day. I looked at those examples and thought being active obviously helps prolong your life. I want to be healthy and agile when I'm 90, so I'm working on it now."

CHAPTER 2 ▶▶▶

There's a guy with a big picture view of his life. He's not just looking at where his life is today, but where he wants to be in the long-term.

When I was a schoolteacher, I remember older teachers leaving the profession for other careers. One colleague left to become a real estate agent, and I thought that was just madness — the whole idea that you would work on something that you didn't get paid for unless you actually produced a result was just a no-no. It seemed like the riskiest thing to do. In fact, no one in my entire family had ever worked for themselves, nor had they considered it. My parents viewed going into business for yourself as the riskiest thing you could do. I mean, my father would rather drink poison then set up shop for himself.

So, I remember thinking about the possibility of being a successful business owner when our part-time business started to produce results. At the same time, the possibility of not being a teacher started to appear over the horizon and I remember thinking, "I've got to do something, otherwise I'll be a teacher for 100 years."

And then one day, I resigned just as it dawned on me: "If I don't put my resignation in today, I'll say I'm going to do it the next day and the next week but I know myself well enough to know that it'll never happen." So I did it.

> "Take a big-picture view of the world."

Then a friend saw me in the school quadrangle one morning and asked me "How you can handle not knowing what's going to happen next year?" And I replied: "How can you handle *knowing* what is going to happen next year?"

I was acting on what people would call 'faith'. But there's more, I think. And that is a belief in the possibility. In handing in my resignation, I was able to move to the next stage: action. I was able to ask "what's next?"

That "what's next" question is the biggie. We change focus from "it can't be done" to "what has to be done?"

The power of positive thinking

In 1988, the optimism guru Dr Martin Seligman worked with the University of California Berkeley swim team to determine which swimmers responded best under adversity and what attitudinal traits were necessary for peak performance. Seligman defined adversity in simple terms: how do people explain their successes and failures to themselves?

> "Both optimism and pessimism are self-fulfilling prophecies."

Dr Seligman has devoted his life to what he calls 'positive psychology' and has found that optimistic people are happier than pessimists. When things go wrong, optimists think of it as temporary, limited in its effect, and not entirely their fault. They see failure as something that can be changed next time around, so that they can succeed. Pessimists do the opposite. They consider the setback to be permanent and far-reaching, assigning it to some lasting characteristic they are helpless to change. These differing explanations have a profound effect on how people respond to life.

Why? Because optimism and pessimism both tend to be self-fulfilling prophecies. Pessimistic explanations tend to be self-defeating, stopping the thinker from taking constructive action to change their circumstances. Optimistic justifications tend to make the thinker more likely to act.

In several large-scale, long-term experiments, Seligman found that optimists are more successful than pessimists — positive politicians win more elections,

CHAPTER 2 ▸▸▸

self-assured students get better grades, confident athletes win more contests and sanguine salespeople make more money.

During his research with the Berkeley swim team, Seligman found that Matt Biondi had one of the most optimistic explanatory styles.

> "Optimism and hope can be learned."

In the Seoul Olympics in 1988, the buzz was that Biondi would win seven gold medals a la Mark Spitz in 1972. Biondi took a disappointing bronze in the first event and, in an apparent mental error, coasted the last metre of the 100-metres butterfly (not his best event) and lost the gold by inches.

While the media predicted a spectacular crash and burn, Seligman sat confident in his lounge room, "because his explanatory style was highly optimistic and he had shown us that he got faster — not slower — after defeat."

Seligman was right: Biondi won gold in the last five events.[24]

While some researchers define optimism as an ability to see the silver lining, and others define it as a personality trait, Seligman suggests that your explanation for why something happens has a major impact on how you will act in the future and what result your actions will bring about. In turn, this has an impact on your self-esteem and self-image.

One source of a positive or negative outlook may well be our inborn temperament, but studies have shown it can be changed with experiences. Optimism and hope can be learned — underlying both is an outlook that psychologists call 'self-efficacy' — the belief that one has mastery over the events of one's life and can meet challenges as they arise.

> When bad things happen:
> - Assume it won't last long;
> - Look around to see what's still working in your life; and
> - Don't blame yourself.
>
> When good things happen:
> - Consider its effects permanent;
> - Examine how your life is positively affected; and
> - Take credit for as much of it as possible!

Rick Snyder from the University of Kansas was also interested in optimism, or more specifically the psychology of hope. In comparing the academic achievements of 3,920 college students, Dr Snyder and his colleagues found that the level of hope among freshmen at the beginning of their first semester was a more accurate predictor of their college grades than were their SAT scores or their grade point averages in high school, the two measures most commonly used to predict college performance.[25]

He explained, "Students with high hope set themselves higher goals and know how to work hard to attain them. When you compare students of equivalent intellectual aptitude on their academic achievements, what sets them apart is hope."

Snyder says it is more than just a sunny view that everything will turn out all right. "It is believing you have both the will and the way to accomplish your goals, whatever they may be."

CHAPTER 2 ▶▶▶

> "When I believe I can, then I acquire the ability to do it even if I didn't have it in the beginning."

What the researchers tell us is that people with high levels of hope share certain traits:

- they can motivate themselves;
- they are resourceful enough to find ways to accomplish their objectives;
- they are flexible enough to find different ways of achieving their goals, or to switch their goals if one becomes impossible; and
- they are able to break down goals into smaller, manageable pieces.

Again, believing it's possible — having hope — means that you will not give in to overwhelming anxiety, a defeatist attitude, or depression in the face of difficult challenges or setbacks. Mahatma Gandhi had it right when he said: "Men often become what they believe themselves to be. If I believe I cannot do something, it makes me incapable of doing it. But when I believe I can, then I acquire the ability to do it even if I didn't have it in the beginning."

Pessimists think that optimists are unrealistic and foolhardy; optimists shake their heads and wonder why people make themselves unnecessarily miserable. So is the glass half-full or half-empty?

Mark Hansen and Robert Allen have a new take on this question in *Cracking the Millionaire Code*. If you're an optimist, you'll say 'half full', while a pessimist will moan 'half empty'. And yet, the answer is neither. The glass is actually 100 per cent full – the bottom half is filled with a visible liquid and the top half is filled with an invisible substance, called air. The glass is actually completely full – it's simply a matter of learning to see the invisible opportunities as well as those in plain sight.[26]

Things to think about...

- Believe in the possibility of achieving your goal. If your goal was possible, what steps would you need to put in place?

- Adopt a possibility-based mind-set that looks for new, different and better ways to attain a goal or solution or address a situation.

- Ask yourself: if goal setting can improve free-throw performance, then what could it do for me?

- The primary purpose of your brain is to do exactly what you tell it to do. So, write your goals down in black and white.

- Learn to speak the language of success. Keep a track of what you say and then change your unsupportive language so that success becomes a natural result of your attitude.

- Remember that actions always speak louder than words, so always do what you say you will.

- Learn to look on the bright side of life. Ask yourself: is the glass half-full or half-empty? If it's half empty, what are you going to do to change your perceptions?

CHAPTER 3
Dump your emotional baggage.

CHAPTER 3 ▸▸▸

To be successful in business, we need to dump our emotional baggage at the door. Many of our greatest business breakthroughs occur in the space between our ears. How we feel about ourselves and the world around us can spark or sabotage our success. For each and every one of us, our single most powerful business tools are our minds, and yet we so often let them be clogged up with old stories, hurts, resentments and ideas about how things 'really are', that there is little chance of success.

When we go into business, we don't slip into a new personality, just like a new suit, the moment we set up shop. Instead, we take ourselves — our personalities, our hang-ups, our mood swings and our emotional baggage with us. Daring to be entrepreneurial is inherently risky. Anyone who has started their own business knows how tough it is to translate an idea into reality — and then make a profit.

In the *E-Myth Revisited*, Michael E Gerber says that your business is nothing more than a distinct reflection of who you are. "If your thinking is sloppy, your business will be sloppy. If you are disorganised, your business will be disorganised. If you are greedy, your employees will be greedy… So if your business is to change — as it must continuously to thrive, you must change first." [27]

> "If your business is to change, you must change first."

So, how do you change?

There is now a considerable body of research suggesting that a person's ability to understand and manage their emotions provides the basis for success in almost all areas of endeavour. So, everything from nurturing a relationship to running a successful business is dependent on your emotional maturity.

It all began about 2,000 years ago when Plato wrote, "All learning has an emotional base." Since then, scientists, educators and philosophers have worked to prove or disprove the importance of feelings. Unfortunately, for a large part of those two millennia, common thought was, "Emotions are in the way. They keep us from making good decisions, and they keep us from focusing." In the last three decades, a growing body of research is proving just the opposite.

> "Intellect cannot work at its best without emotional intelligence."

When researchers Peter Salovey and John Mayer coined the term "emotional intelligence" in 1990, they described emotional intelligence as "a form of social intelligence that involves the ability to monitor one's own and others' feelings and emotions, to discriminate among them, and to use this information to guide one's thinking and action".

Daniel Goleman, in his book *Emotional Intelligence*, says "we have two different kinds of intelligence: rational and emotional. How we do in life is determined by both – it is not just IQ, but emotional intelligence that matters. Indeed, intellect cannot work at its best without emotional intelligence."[28]

IQ by itself is not a very good predictor of job performance. Goleman's research indicates that only 20 per cent of your success is the result of your IQ, with another 36 per cent attributable to your EQ. At least 90 per cent of the difference between outstanding and average leaders is related to EQ and explains why some people excel while others of the same calibre lag behind.

Here's an example. A 40-year longitudinal investigation of 450 boys who grew up in Sommerville, Massachusetts, found that IQ is not necessarily a predictor

CHAPTER 3 ▸▸▸

of success. Two-thirds of the boys were from welfare families, and one-third had IQs below 90. However, IQ had little relation to how well they did at work or in the rest of their lives. What made the biggest difference were childhood abilities such as being able to handle frustration, control emotions, and get along with other people.[29]

So, having a high emotional intelligence will help you achieve the business and life outcomes you want and deserve. To harmonise our head and heart, we must understand how to use emotions intelligently. As Goleman says, emotional intelligence is "being able to motivate oneself and persist in the face of frustration; to control impulse and delay gratification, to regulate our moods and keep distress from swamping our ability to think, to empathise and to hope" — all those things crucial to business success.

We also should keep in mind that skills of the head and skills of the heart are very much related. In fact, in the famous 'marshmallow studies' at Stanford University which I mentioned in Chapter 1, ten years later the kids who were able to resist temptation had a total SAT score that was 210 points higher than those kids who were unable to wait.

> "High emotional intelligence will help you achieve the business and life outcomes you want and deserve."

And here's how the marshmallow test plays out later in life: I see a lot of people who would love to be in business for themselves, but they can't get started because they can't find the funds. It staggers me to think that they don't have the ability to go without pay for a couple of months while they get going. Does that mean they aren't able to save such a small amount to set them on the journey to their dreams?

The emotional brain

In the last fifty years or so, neurologists have come to the conclusion that our brain is 'three-tiered' and that each tier forms a different centre of awareness. The three types are identified as the Cortex (responsible for language, thinking, planning, organising and consciousness), the brainstem and cerebellum (dedicated to movement, physical senses and instinctual responses) and the limbic system — the emotional centre of the brain.

Although we may not realise it, much of what we do is an attempt to manage mood. The limbic system employs a structure of reward and punishment, which is expressed as feelings of expansion and contraction. In all of our experiences of wellbeing, the overwhelming sense is of expansion of consciousness, of feeling limitless and free. Unfortunately, we often experience its polar opposite, a sense of being imprisoned and inadequate.

Of course we embrace the feeling of expanding consciousness. And we find ways of kick-starting the mood. Some people do it through mind-altering drugs or alcohol, others through sex, money or power. Some do it through risking their body in sports. Others by playing the stock market or gambling on the horses.

As Goleman says: "The design of the brain means that we very often have little or no control over when we are swept by emotion, nor over what emotion it will be. But we can have some say in how long an emotion will last."

> "We often have little or no control over when we are swept by emotion, but we can have some say in how long an emotion will last."

For most of us who struggle with our emotions, suppression is the solution. If we want to suppress an emotion, we have to actively do so. We develop techniques to hold

CHAPTER 3 ▶▶▶

the energy within our system; we either detach (either physically, mentally or emotionally), distract ourselves (by being busy, working hard, rushing, watching TV) or we alter our moods.

Addictions form as we become reliant on suppressive behaviours to maintain our inner sense of control, comfort and stability. An addiction is a powerful (some say pathological) emotional need to create a 'mood altering experience', despite the life damaging consequence of that very same experience.

> "An addiction is a powerful (some say pathological) emotional need to create a 'mood altering experience'."

When we look at what mood needs to be altered, we find one of life's worst feelings — shame. Bound up inside its many layers, shame often carries large doses of hurt and loneliness. Because we know so little about the existence of these feelings buried deep inside us, we are not aware that they surreptitiously surface in our daily lives and begin to drive us. Imagine a submarine that you cannot see, let alone discern clearly or define with a name.

The daily battle to earn enough 'brownie points' to build a positive self-image draws our awareness away from self-knowledge (I am hurt, I am lonely, I am not good enough) and towards the external trappings of success. The greater this external success, the more effective it is at disguising the lurking submarine. Typically we hear in our clinical work, "Who me? Poor self-image! You must be joking!"

What the addict needs to admit before any kind of cure is possible is that there are life-damaging consequences of their actions — and that these things happen repeatedly. The most common example in our culture is the alcoholic who claims that they do not have a problem; meanwhile hundreds of thousands of undiagnosed addicts walk the streets. The most common go almost unnoticed — the person not complete without a partner; the shopaholic; the workaholic; the chocaholic and the sex addict.

Common to all addictions is the need to indulge in them as a means of making the shame from the last dose disappear. Imagine the gambler, broke and desperate, who can stave off the feelings of shame by getting another bet on. "If I could just get this winner home," he says as he briefly alters his mood. Picture the chocaholic, feeling fat and slovenly, all the while shovelling chocolate into her mouth. See the workaholic, who suppresses his feelings of inadequacy by concentrating on his career. Or the shopaholic, shameful about the last spree, who nevertheless feels the rush when she gets out the credit card to splurge at the sales.

What the addict wants to avoid by indulging once again is, in fact, the solution. It is in feeling both the sources, and the current level of, these emotions — deeply, fully and probably repeatedly — that salvation lies. Usually this is too gut-wrenchingly terrifying for them to consider, let alone attempt.

While it is easy to say that most addicts are too scared to look inside themselves for fear of what they might find, the reality is that they are mostly totally unaware of their addiction. They have it rationalised. How about you?

> "Most people are totally unaware of their addiction. How about you?"

Clear the emotional clutter

It is important to realise that just because we do not feel or express any emotional energy outwardly, does not mean the energy was not created. Once an emotion has been generated within our bodies, it

CHAPTER 3 ▸▸▸

will not go away until we allow it to be felt and expressed. If we restrict the expression of an emotion, energy will be stored at a cellular level in our bodies. In this way, our bodies act as containers for unexpressed emotional energy. As we suppress our emotions, we build up reservoirs within our bodies. Arthur Janov, founder of 'Primal Therapy', called these reservoirs 'primal pools' of emotion.[30] Janov proposed that there are four primal pools of emotion:

- Sadness
- Fear
- Anger
- Joy

I think there are actually two more primal pools:

- Shame
- Guilt

> "To master our emotions, we need to know how to identify and then handle our feelings."

As we suppress an emotion, it gets added to the pool of its type. For example, as we suppress our anger, it gets added to the reservoir of unexpressed anger that we are carrying around in our bodies.

It is inevitable that these stores of unexpressed emotion will surface one way or another. Just as the submarine must eventually come up for air and supplies, our lives (our actions or even our bodies) will ultimately reflect these storehouses of suppression.

To master our emotions, we need to know how to identify and then handle our feelings. This can mean getting more closely in touch with anger, fear and grief, and being able to express them at the right moment.

How you handle feelings of anger and fear influences how you live your life and whom you spend it with. We often gradually limit our world to one where anger and fear never arise. If a lot of the fear and anger that we are trying to avoid is actually our own, we can't develop emotional intelligence until we accept it and deal with it.

> **"Emotions have two related origins: the body and its history."**

While there is still a great deal of uncertainty about our emotions — and scientists have only just skimmed the surface of the emotional brain — we know emotions have two related origins: the body and its history. Many present-day feelings are relics from the past. When we encounter threat, pleasure or pain in the present, old feelings of distress, coupled with what we did to survive the stress, may be restimulated.

Events in the present that echo a painful earlier experience arouse the old distress recorded in the body and mind, together with the corresponding defensive strategy that we adopted to survive. For example, if we experienced a painful separation from a parent as a young child and responded by forgetting the pain, then in adult life parting from someone close to us is likely to reactivate the memory, so that the adult separation may become an emotional disaster. The bigger the array of early painful memories, the greater will be the number of events in the present that are likely to trigger them. Not surprisingly, we all go to some trouble to avoid potentially reactivating events.

Whenever we encounter a painful threat or a pleasurable experience, our mind absorbs the information and acts autonomously. For example, when someone close to us is hurt we may feel a lump in our throat or tears, when a baby is born we find ourselves smiling. The feelings happen, but we only become aware of them retrospectively through our thoughts.

CHAPTER 3 ▸▸▸

We have no choice about our spontaneous feelings but we can choose how to act on them. A friend arrives unexpectedly and is obviously upset. We have urgent work to finish and feel irritated and anxious about that, but sad about our friend. We are not responsible for these feelings. They happen. But we have a choice. We can act on the sadness and help our friend, we can tell her we are too busy, or we can tell her we are annoyed that she arrived without phoning first.

When our needs are not fully met as children, our body and mind respond emotionally and store the memory of those feelings. To cope with these feelings we defend ourselves in a way that seems appropriate at the time. This survival decision is also stored in our memory banks. See the diagram below

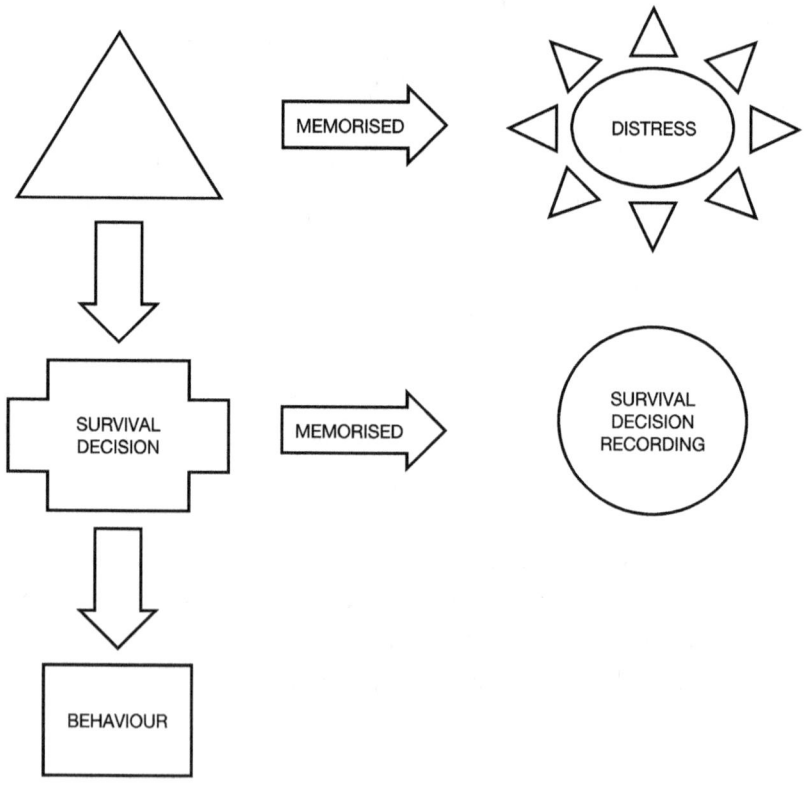

As an adult, when an event occurs which reminds us of the earlier difficulties, it evokes the original feelings of distress stored in our body and mind. We then have a choice: we can decide to respond appropriately, and reject the influence of the earlier survival decision, or we can allow the earlier survival decision to recur automatically so that we continue to behave inappropriately.

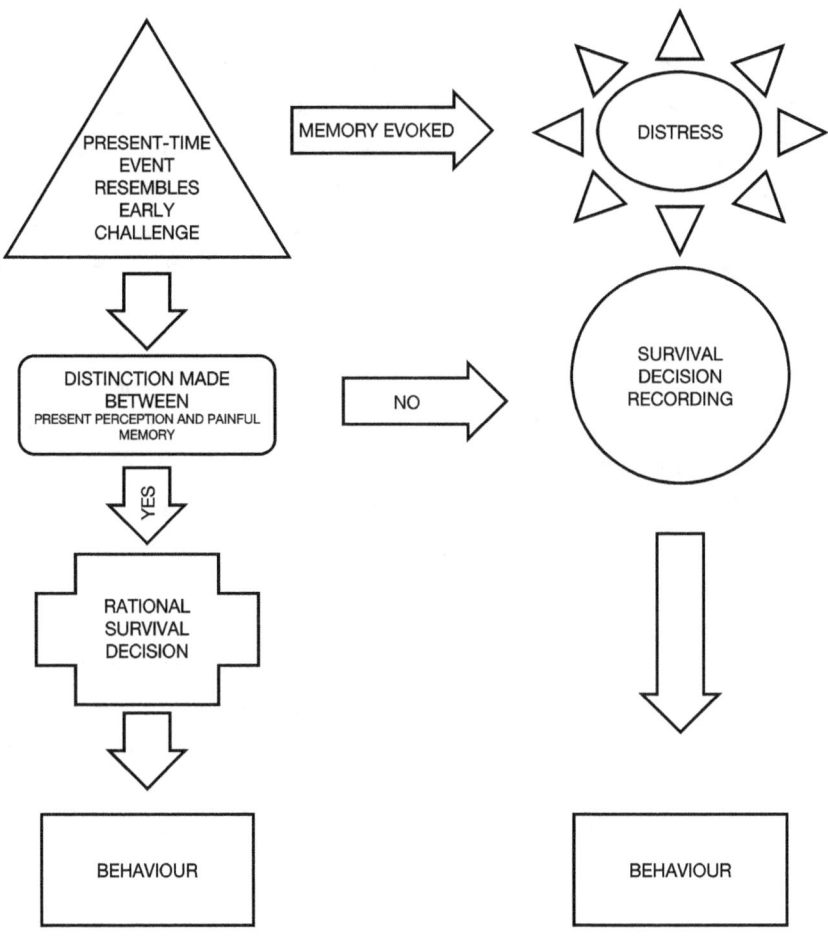

CHAPTER 3 ▸▸▸

Lightening the load

In *Emotional Alchemy*, Tara Bennett-Goleman writes that "Becoming aware of emotional patterns gives us an idea of where our attachments are, so that we have a more precise awareness of the emotional patterns that motivate us."[31]

> **"Explicit memories are not carbon copies of the experiences that created them."**

Even though a memory of an emotional experience is strong and vivid, it is not necessarily accurate. Explicit memories, regardless of their emotional implications, are not carbon copies of the experiences that created them. They are reconstructions at the time of recall, and the state of the brain at the time of the recall can influence the way in which the withdrawn memory is remembered.

Research has shown that the memory is also vulnerable to being modified by events that take place after the memory was formed. For example, Brigadier General Thorpe, who witnessed the bombing of Pearl Harbour, described the event one way at the time of his retirement but had given a different version in an earlier memoir. Both of these accounts had many inconsistencies with information from other sources.

Another example is provided by research examining people's memories of the explosion of the space shuttle Challenger at two times — the day after and several years later. Most of the subjects said their memories of what they were doing when they heard the news were very good. Yet, in many instances, the memory at the later time was very different from the memory reported the day after.

These examples and many others suggest we should have, according to neuroscientist Joseph LeDoux, "a healthy suspicion of the accuracy of explicit memories of emotional situations when the details have important consequences." [32]

In fact, in our clinical work over the years, we have noticed something quite revealing about memory. We don't really remember an event as it was — we remember the feeling of it as we last recalled it.

We typically see clients recalling a twenty year old memory and realising that they have modified it marginally at each anniversary by as little as 1 or 2 per cent — resulting in a 30–40 per cent falsification that they honestly believe to be true.

You have probably already had the insight that, as far as emotions are concerned, we need to experience them fully, completely and unreservedly. While our culture tells us that some emotions (particularly anger, sadness and fear) are unacceptable, hurtful to others or just downright nasty, these unexpressed emotions can lodge themselves in our psyches, making it physically difficult to move on and grow.

> "There are always consequences when you resist your feelings."

The healing is in the feeling

If you want to resist your feelings, that's fine as long as you realise there will be consequences. For example, have you ever been furious with the boss at work, yet couldn't tell him or her how angry you felt? Then on the drive home, you notice that every bad driver in town is cutting in and out dangerously in front of your car? When you get home, your husband has left his tools out in the

CHAPTER 3 ▸▸▸

> "There is a definite limit to the amount of emotion that we can hold within our bodies before it breaks out."

front yard. You have asked him over and over again not to do this. He receives a blast of your anger — which includes the anger at your boss, plus the road rage on your way home from work. Later you end up feeling guilty.

The consequences of suppressing our emotions are that we end up hurting others and ourselves. We lose our energy and feel fatigued all the time. We diminish our ability to feel all our emotions — so not only do we suppress our anger, fear and sadness, but our love, peace and joy too. And as we detach from our feelings, we lose touch with our inner strength and feelings of self-confidence.

There is a definite limit to the amount of emotion that we can hold within our bodies (and still continue to function) before it breaks out. It can break out physically, mentally or emotionally. Suppressed emotional energy breaks out:

- **Physically** as illness and disease
- **Mentally** as confusion and mental breakdowns
- **Emotionally** as arguments, depression and emotional breakdowns.

The word 'emotion' is perplexing. A contraction of the much more enlightening expression, 'energy in motion', this simple phrase suggests what we should be doing with emotions — expressing them. Yet, this is the very thing we avoid and the thing that has caused modern humanity so much pain.

We all feel our emotions in our bodies — heart-thumping love, gut-wrenching fear or fist-clenching anger. Yet, our training has been to 'reason' with our emotions — to push our feelings into our heads so we can 'work them out'. We want to know where to place them, what we should do with them, or how we should change them for more socially acceptable versions.

In most cases, this leads to active suppression of our feelings; resulting at best with a feeling of blankness, and at worst with uncontrolled outbursts. Typically, as thinkers, we want to reason our way through our unfathomable actions, wondering why we are unable to control our emotions in the way we would like.

> **"You can't think your way through a feeling."**

Step number one for anyone who wants to gain emotional mastery is to understand that our emotions are real. They are an energy force that needs to be expressed, despite their 'social acceptability'. We just need to find safe ways to 'get it out' instead of 'bottling it up'.

As I say every time I get the chance in a workshop: "You can't think your way through a feeling."

Part of the process of learning emotional expression is realising that we do not dislike the 'bad' emotions themselves (anger, sadness and fear), but the ugly, mean, vengeful or manipulative way in which we have seen them used in the past. So, it is not anger that we fear. It is the violence which so many people display when angry that really bothers us. The violence, or threat of it, can cause fear — especially within those who have been on the receiving end of it in the past. As Aristotle wisely said: "Anyone can be angry — that is easy. But to be angry with the right person, to the right degree, at the right time, for the right purpose, and in the right way — this is not easy."

Step two in the process of emotional empowerment is to take responsibility for how we feel. Often, we blame outside forces, 'the comedian made me laugh', we say, 'she made me angry' — we accuse others of being responsible for our feelings. The result? We turn ourselves into powerless victims.

CHAPTER 3 ▸▸▸

Rather than buy into the idea that we are powerless and that our emotions are out of our control, we need to become emotionally adept.

While our feelings are real, they are quite often created by totally unreal judgements, reactions and perceptions that we don't recognise. That being the case, we mistakenly assume that we can't help how we feel. We feel we have no control over our emotions.

Feelings are energy moving through our bodies. This energy naturally seeks expression and our major difficulties are encountered when it is blocked. Obviously bottled emotions don't just go away. They can be made to subside, allowing us to behave more like trained animals than humans, but the cost of this suppression will require a lifetime of repayments.

> "80 per cent of the patients in our hospitals are there for stress-related illnesses."

Medical experts now tell us that up to 80 per cent of the patients in our hospitals are there because of a stress-related illness. In all likelihood, stressed by the never-ending effort expended in suppressing feelings that need to be released. My observation is that people who find life heavy going spend much of their daily energy on suppressing emotions that they cannot find a way to safely express: the anger of past abuse; the deep sorrow of a child's death; the fear of an unknown future. With so much energy being channelled into emotional suppression, is it any wonder why being 'tired all the time' has become so common that doctors now use the universal acronym TATT?

This syndrome is known as the 'internal battle' — a battle that rages away constantly while everything on the surface seems serene.

This emotional suppression blunts our experience of our vibrant wellbeing.

We need to master our emotions, not suppress them. We need to learn how to heal ourselves from emotional hurt, and we need to make a habit of putting this learning into practice in everyday life. Although the causes of our hurts are wide-ranging (everything from childhood abuse, school bullying, failed exams, redundancy and marriage break-ups to put-downs from colleagues and friends) our blocks to healing and the treatment we needed to overcome these are very similar. The solution is simple: the healing is in the feeling.

And in dumping your emotional baggage, in learning to experience all your emotions, you will, in the words of Friedrich Nietzsche "become the person you truly are." [33]

> **Case Study:**
> **Emotional mastery is worth more than money**
>
> One of Jason Urbanowicz's earliest memories is of being five years old and watching his father become increasingly frustrated by his inability to understand his times tables.
>
> "In an instant, my confidence was shaken, and I made a decision about myself," Jason says. "I decided that I wasn't any good at academic pursuits. And from that moment on, I found school a struggle. I remember feeling like I had to 'pretend' my way through school and hope that no one would find out that I wasn't intelligent."
>
> While it was possible to muddle his way through high school, soon the big wide world loomed. "And how will I bluff my way through that?" Jason remembers thinking.

CHAPTER 3 ▸▸▸

"I went down to the local job search office, scanned the job boards and found a wood machinist apprenticeship there for the taking. I thought maybe that sort of job would match my intelligence and that I'd manage to get by OK."

Despite 20 applicants, Jason got the job. He hated every second of his three years choking on sawdust and working for peanuts. Eventually fate stepped in and Jason's boss went broke. Jason was cut loose, and with some experience in martial arts, soon drifted into security work.

"After four years as a bouncer, I found myself standing out the front of a nightclub on a Saturday night, watching people get drunk and asking myself: how did my life end up like this?"

Again, fate intervened and Jason was embroiled in a two-year court case after an altercation in a nightclub. He lost his security licence, and gained a three-year good behaviour bond in the process. "The judge gave me a taste of gaol by locking me up for a couple of weeks, and that was enough for me. While I wasn't happy about it at the time, I thank the judge for it every day now!"

Looking for a fresh start, Jason moved from his hometown of Brisbane to Melbourne. "You can run away, but you can't get away!" he explains. "I took all my problems along with me to Melbourne — and added the extra stress of not knowing anyone and not having any direction."

Jason went from job to job, working on factory floors and back at the front doors of nightclubs, always trying to ignore that nagging voice in the back of his head, which asked: "What am I doing? Why can't I get what I want from life?"

His weight ballooned from 105 to 153 kilos in less than two years, and his confidence was at its lowest ebb.

"Eventually, I decided I had had enough and it was up to me to turn my life around," Jason says. "I asked myself: if I did one thing, what would get me the best results the quickest? I knew how to get into shape, and I knew I'd gain confidence and energy for being fit, so I started training."

And turn his life around he did. Jason's commitment landed him an Australian body building title – a huge achievement. "But although my physical appearance had changed, I still felt the same inside. Nothing about me had really changed except my muscle condition."

He moved again, this time back to Brisbane to open a gym with a friend. Another six months of trials and tribulations followed, and the business folded. Forklift driving, and time studying to be a personal trainer were the next career changes along the road.

But with his qualifications and a drive to achieve, Jason became a very successful personal trainer, earning more than $100k a year. And yet, he was still looking for something, and realised that before he could truly help other people, he needed to overcome the personal blockages that were holding him back.

CHAPTER 3 ▸▸▸

"Along came Paul Blackburn, who I met through a mutual friend, and I started coaching," Jason says. "I learnt how to drop the old baggage that would hijack me and how to recognise when I was making decisions based on my old programs. Essentially, I learned how to my master emotions in the same way I'd learned to master the weights equipment at the gym."

Since then, Jason's career has changed course again – this time he's established a success coaching business in Queensland, and he's on track to make a million dollars this year.

"The person that I've become is more important to me than the money I've earned," he concludes. "Five years ago, I wondered whether I'd ever achieve anything with my life. And now, the world is my oyster."[34]

Things to think about...

- Our success in life is determined by both our mental and emotional intelligence. Improving your emotional intelligence is one of the best business decisions you can make.

- Don't buy into the idea that you are powerless and that your emotions are out of our control. Become aware of your emotional patterns and learn to identify your triggers.

- Be bold and brave. Ask yourself: what are my addictions? How am I going to face them and overcome them, rather than simply rationalising them?

- Many present-day feelings are relics from the past. Ask yourself: what steps will I take to clear my emotional clutter?

- The healing is in the feeling. You can't think your way through a feeling. How are you going to express yourself?

CHAPTER 4
Face your fears.

CHAPTER 4 ▸▸▸

In 1995, Nelson Mandela published *Long Walk to Freedom*, in which he described his 27 years of incarceration during the struggle against apartheid in South Africa.

Eighteen of those 27 years were spent on the notorious Robben Island, where he and other prisoners performed hard labour in a lime quarry. Prison conditions were basic in the extreme, with black prisoners receiving the harshest treatment and the fewest rations. Mandela describes how, as a D-group prisoner (the lowest classification) he was permitted just one visitor and one letter every six months. When they did arrive, letters were often delayed for long periods and made indecipherable by the prison censors.[35]

> "The brave man is not he who does not feel afraid, but he who conquers that fear."

For most of us, such tremendous hardship — both physical and mental — is unfathomable. Perhaps even more astounding is Mandela's assertion that "I learned that courage was not the absence of fear, but the triumph over it. The brave man is not he who does not feel afraid, but he who conquers that fear."

A fear of public speaking, spiders, snakes, talking to strangers, flying or failing in business just doesn't come close to the fears that Nelson Mandela faced while imprisoned on Robben Island.

So, what fear could be stopping you from the success that you deserve?

The belief that businesses are more likely to fail than succeed leads many people to skip the entrepreneurial experience, and the satisfaction and freedom that it brings. In fact, the tragedy of modern life is that the masses of people lead what Henry David Thoreau called "lives of quiet desperation".[36] Far too many people go to their graves with songs that were never written, pictures that were never painted, businesses that were never built, and troubled hearts that never experienced joy. The reason? Fear. The problem is we become fearful about things that turn out to be nothing at all.

A story from the Indian scriptures aptly illustrates this:

> It was midnight in a small village in India, and a man was walking down the very dark and unlit road to his home. This region was notorious for its dangerous and deadly snakes and the man was already very frightened as he walked tremulously along the path. "What if I encounter a snake?" he worried, wavering at the simple thought of a poisonous serpent.
>
> Suddenly, in the gloom, the man noticed something long and thick coiled up in the middle of the road. "It's a snake!" he shouted. "Help! Help! Someone come quickly! I'm about to be killed by a snake!"
>
> Another villager heard the man's cry, and ran towards the sound of the shouting.
>
> "What's the matter?" he asked.
>
> "Look! Look!" yelped the first man, pointing a trembling finger at the coiled-up serpent. "It's a snake!"
>
> The second villager cautiously approached the shadow in the road, held up his lantern and looked. And there before him was the coil of thick rope that someone had accidentally dropped on the path.

> **"What fear could be stopping you from the success that you deserve?"**

CHAPTER 4 ▶▶▶

"There is no snake here," the villager said soothingly, "only a rope. Fear has made your mind play a trick on you."

How many times have you mistaken a rope for a snake in your own life? You run around, stirred up by your fear and lose your peace of mind — all you had to do was look more carefully at what appeared to be a snake and discover it was only an illusion. This is how fear drains your energy and immobilises you. I'm fond of pointing out to students in my workshops that fear is nothing more than:

False
Expectation
Appearing
Real

> **"The secret to working with fear is to make your courage bigger than your fear."**

The snake appeared to be real, but it wasn't. Life will always be full of ropes that appear to be snakes.

In psychology, a common breakdown of the time we spend on various worries goes something like this:

Things that will never happen	40%
Things that are in the past	30%
Needless concerns about one's health	12%
Petty and miscellaneous cares	10%
Real and legitimate concerns	8%

Of the 8 per cent of worries that are real and legitimate, half of them are about things we cannot influence. So the solution is not to try to dispel your fear but to deal with it differently. Remember Nelson Mandela's words. The secret to working with fear is to make your courage bigger than your fear.

We do this by turning compassionately towards the fear in order to examine it, to explore it, to understand it. Not, as the oft-heard expression says, to confront it (as the result will be even more traumatic), but to 'be' with it long enough for its grip on us to loosen.

I've discovered that this process will work for even the most terrified person. At workshops attended by as many as 1,000 people, using this technique, I have been able to get someone afraid of speaking in public to take stage and present alongside me in less than a few minutes.

As we grow and face change, it is inevitable that we experience some fear. All growth includes struggles and victories, and when the growth is personal, the battles occur inside you. This inner battle that you experience as you make your way in life is a battle between your fear of moving forward and the courage to do it.

> **"All growth includes struggles and victories, and when the growth is personal, the battles occur inside you."**

To understand how to win the battle with fear, we need to understand the true source of fear. And like everything, it starts when we are children.

Small children have very few fears. As they learn to walk, talk, explore and try new things, they do so with passion and enthusiasm and complete absence of fear. Any mother will tell you that her toddler tearaway is 'fearless' as he climbs ladders, leaps from trees and hurtles across the road without a care.

But then one day, that child is hurt. It may be the first time he hears the word 'no' from a parent; perhaps it is when he is physically injured (only a matter of time with all that climbing and leaping); maybe it happens if someone yells at him.

CHAPTER 4 ▸▸▸

Regardless of when this event occurs, whether at six months or six years old, it has the same effect: the child experiences pain and, like most human beings, hates it and does everything he can to avoid experiencing it again.

And so, instead of clambering up the next ladder he spies, the little boy is tentative. His fear is successful in preventing him from doing what his mind thought could hurt him (based on the ones that hurt in the past). The source of fear is, therefore, not self-hatred or low self-esteem — fear is simply a protective mechanism.

The trouble is that it ends up protecting us from happiness as well. Many times our fear thinks something is dangerous when it isn't. Really, there is just something vaguely familiar about the situation that reminds us of a time in the past when we were in emotional danger.

Many of us know we have fear in certain areas of our life, but we also allow fear to hold us back in some very subtle ways. Perhaps you put off starting a difficult task until the last minute, because you fear you won't do a good enough job. You might avoid a colleague who you know is upset with you because you don't want to be confronted. Or perhaps you tell yourself that your dreams and goals aren't really that important, rather than admitting your frustration that you're not achieving them.

> **"Fear suppresses your productivity, decision making ability, creativity and - believe it or not - success itself."**

The more fear controls your decisions and behaviour, the more it drains you of your energy, your enthusiasm and your passion for life. What's more, fear suppresses your productivity, decision making ability, creativity and — believe it or not — success itself.

Fear is like an emotional roommate that lives with you day and night. It talks to you, manipulates you and tries to convince you to avoid doing or expressing anything that may cause you any kind of discomfort or involve any sort of risk. It says, "you can't", and "you shouldn't". It eats away at your confidence and your self-esteem.

So, what do we need to do? Fear thrives in darkness; so if you think there's a bogeyman under the bed, turn on the light.

Farewell the fear of failure

When Classical Greek armies sailed across the seas to battle, the first thing they would do upon landing was to burn their boats, leaving them stranded and facing the enemy. Failure was then not an option. Only victory assured them a safe passage home.

> "What if you set yourself a target and you don't reach it?"

The fear of failing is a very real fear in every human being, despite what some of the outwardly brave ones will tell you. Have you ever thought to yourself, "what if I set a target and I don't reach it?"

For some people, their fear of failure drives them to actually have a go because they don't want to fail. For them, it's not difficult to start something because they are motivated to move forward rather than risk failure. I know a very successful sales person, for instance, who said he was terrified of making cold calls. Eventually, he was spurred into action by an even greater fear – the fear of failing, of losing his business and of losing his livelihood.

For other people, the fear of failure is immobilising. They don't want to fail,

CHAPTER 4 ▸▸▸

so they don't move. For some people, fear — from fear of spiders, to heights, to public speaking, to death, and everything in between – paralyses. Someone with a fear of heights, when placed on the edge of the cliff, will stand stiff with fear. And when paralysis hits, nothing happens. No action, no result.

Most of us have a nagging fear (some conscious, others subconscious) of failing. If we fail, we will prove ourselves less worthwhile than appearances suggest. Not only will we feel unworthy, but perhaps everybody watching us will come to the same awful conclusion.

> "Most of us are terrified of trying something new because we risk failure."

Why do we feel this way? Because our society teaches us that we are not lovable and worthwhile because of who we are, but because of the things that we do.

In an ideal world, our sense of self would be a balance of who we are and what we do. We'd know that our successes, career achievements and possessions are great, but are only part of who we are. In times of trial, when our sense of self eludes us, it's great to have a track record to fall back on — we can reflect on all those achievements and accumulations and remind ourselves that we're OK, that we've made a contribution, that we're doing a good job. Conversely, when we have a failure and our track record looks grim, our deep and abiding feelings of being good enough, just the way we are, allows us to take failure in our stride.

Unfortunately, for most of us, our sense of identity is more likely to come almost entirely from what we do; we have no understanding of who we are without our success. As a result, most of us are terrified of trying something new because we risk failure, and therefore risk what we think is the very core of ourselves.

This belief that "we are what we do" is simple when you consider the first time you ever washed up or folded your own clothes. It was probably a cause for congratulations and approval in your home. Parents wanting to teach their children basic social skills use positive reinforcement to convey the idea that the accomplishment is highly desirable. Small children see that they are pleasing the most important people in their world by what they do, rather than understand that they are loved anyway. Of course, we see the opposite as well: parents wanting to ensure that their children do not repeat an undesirable act will express some kind of disapproval, whether it be anger, condemnation, disappointment or stony silence.

Young minds often presume that they are not loved when they do things that are 'wrong' or 'not good'. As a result, they make one of two conclusions:

NUMBER ONE: "If I try something and fail, I will prove I'm not good enough and they won't love me"; or

NUMBER TWO: "If I do something good, they will love me more".

The fear of failure becomes a protective mechanism to ensure they don't get hurt, lose love or feel inadequate.

> **"The fear of failure is often a protective mechanism to avoid hurt."**

People who are afraid to set goals and targets almost certainly have internalised belief number one. These people would rather not attempt to achieve something worthwhile, because there is a chance that they will fail and this will be perceived as 'not good'. There can be no punishment greater for the owner of this program than to feel that they have been seen as 'not good', because they know the result of being 'not good' is that love will be taken away from them.

CHAPTER 4 ▶▶▶

And so, we have the fear of failure. It's not actually the failure that we fear; it is the consequences of failure that are so scary and immobilising.

When we fail, by far the worst thing that happens to us is that we judge ourselves. We decide that we are less worthwhile, deserving, whole or complete because of the failure. This final and unchangeable decision about ourselves is the root cause of all poor self images.

Why unchangeable?

Because nobody is there to argue the toss. In the quiet of our own minds we can make any decision we like — and we do.

Our sense of failure is most pervasive whenever we reach down, call upon our strengths, and they are found wanting. Despite society's well-intentioned advice to "try and try again," a little voice in our heads says, "I identified a talent, cultivated it into a strength, claimed it, practiced it and still failed! You really are no good."

> "It's not actually the failure that we fear; it is the consequences of failure that are so scary."

People with belief number two have what I like to call "Approval by Achievement Syndrome". These people are trapped on the dizzy merry-go-round of gaining, achieving, making, doing; they are hooked on the need for positive results. A failure means that they are no good; a stuff-up is proof that they are not OK and a fractured relationship is proof that they are inadequate.

Of course, if we were actually able to achieve all our goals one year (and be silly enough to think better of ourselves as a result) we'd be required to do more the next year just to stay level. Having to do more to be more results in what I call the "series of escalating goals". This becomes a life script.

Unfortunately we won't recognise it until we are at least 35 or 40 years old and by then, achievement has become a habit that feels 'natural'.

This series of escalating goals leads to the Approval by Achievement Syndrome, a situation where we will only like ourselves when we are successful.

The need to be continually achieving, winning and better than others is exhausting, because it's impossible to sustain. It is extremely unlikely that any one person can be better than all the other 6.6 billion people in the world at anything. If we feel we have to be better than somebody else, rather than just being the best we can, we are doomed to be a constant failure until the day we die. Even Tiger Woods, a man who is probably better at golf than every other person on the planet, is focused on improving himself rather than looking around at who he's beaten. "You can always become better," he says.

While success is probably more fun than failure, we need to understand that we are enough. Full stop. Anyone who loves us will sooner or later arrive at this conclusion. Our actions and results may positively or negatively affect them but if they truly love us, they will look beyond the external façade and see who we are amid our victories and failures.

> "It is extremely unlikely that any one person can be better than all the other 6.6 billion people in the world at anything."

We need to do the same for ourselves.

Whatever you do, all achievements — large or small — contribute to your sense of self-worth. How you value these achievements is what's important. If

CHAPTER 4 ▸▸▸

you tend to base your sense of personal value on success, don't be surprised if you feel upset at the prospect of failure or anxious that you may be rejected.

The fear of failure hurts far more than the failure itself. Most of us can learn to accept and deal with the worst if we really know what's coming. We may not like it or look forward to it, but we can handle it. Not knowing is a different story. It creates anxiety, vacillation and a very gut level desire to escape the whole problem.

In my family, being in business for oneself was akin to drinking poison. My parents celebrated when I became a schoolteacher because I had found a job I couldn't lose. I grew up with their financial mentality, which was fear of uncertainty. My parents worked hard and watched their pennies, raised four children well and lived decently. But with no life experience outside those gained in jobs, they accepted terrible financial advice in retirement from moneymen who robbed them blind. Just recently, one advisor told them to place $50,000 dollars into an organisation that went broke the next day. Clearly, the lack of experience with investing and risking has cost them more than it would have done, had they had a go at running a local delicatessen or selling real estate or running a caravan park for a while.

> **"The fear of failure hurts far more than the failure itself."**

Or better still, if they had confronted their beliefs and learned a bit about investing, the $50K loss would have been avoided altogether. Their decision that they were merely 'working people' who knew nothing about the financial world may have come from the evidence gathered during their working lives, but it cost them dearly to run with that belief rather than confront it.

> "Act, learn, refine, act, learn, refine - this is the essence of living."

So, you dare to dream, take a gamble and it doesn't pay off. You face the worst consequences of failure and you fail to perform to your expectations. Yes, it hurts, but it shouldn't undermine you completely. It is a chance to learn and to incorporate this learning into your next performance, and the next. And what if these next performances still fail to meet your standards? Well, it hurts some more. But it should also tell you something: you might be searching for your strengths in the wrong places. Despite the hurt, you are at least freed up to redirect your search more productively.

This advice may be difficult to put into practice, but as you build your strengths, achieve your goals and grow as a person, sometimes making great progress, sometimes slipping back, take comfort from the fact that this is how life is supposed to be lived. This process — act, learn, refine, act, learn, refine — clumsy though it may be, is the essence of living.

Case study
From the jaws of fear to success

From childhood hang-ups to work worries, Steven Spielberg is a living example of the success that is possible when you move beyond your fears and focus instead on your goals.

"He was scared of just about everything," recalls Spielberg's mother. "When trees brushed against the house, he would head into my bed."

CHAPTER 4 ▸▸▸

As Spielberg remembers it: "I was afraid of small spaces and I was afraid of the tree outside my window, and I had all these phobias. I think many kids have those phobias, but I probably had more than most."

In 1957, the Spielbergs moved to Scottsdale, Arizona, where they were the only Jewish family in the neighbourhood.

"It's one of those things that I always hate to admit, but I was ashamed of being so different," Spielberg says. "And I was ashamed of my grandfather calling me by my Hebrew name, Schmuel.

"And he would also speak in Yiddish," he adds. "I think I was just a very insecure kid, and I put a big magnifying glass up to myself and said, 'You know, I'm not as good as anybody else'."

But then he discovered he was good at making movies. Since winning Best Picture for Jaws in 1975, Spielberg has brought the world Indiana Jones, E.T, Close Encounters of the Third Kind, Schindler's List, Gremlins and The Colour Purple.

To this day, Spielberg is panic-stricken by his movie premieres and cannot manage to sit through movie previews himself. "My stomach can't take it," he says.

While he still experiences fear, these days he uses it to his advantage. "I still have pretty much the same fears I had growing up," he says. "I've carried them with me right through my life until now. And I'm not sure I want to give those up because I think a lot of those insecurities are fuel for the stories that I tell."[37]

Learn to fail well

Part of the key to success in business is learning to fail well. And yet, how many people can lose a big business deal and say, "That was great. I learned something from it and am better for it"? Unless we can say it — and really mean it — we probably weren't learning that much from the experience.

It may come as a surprise to hear that truly successful people and organisations have not only failed, but have been good at failing. An apt illustration is the salesman who knows that for every sale he makes he will get ten rejections. If he starts his day with a rejection, he can say, "I'm probably not going to be able to do anything today, so I might as well knock off," or he can say, "One down, only nine to go until I make my sale." The second attitude will keep him on the job longer with a much more satisfying feeling and better sales.

Senator Robert Kennedy once said that "only those who dare to fail greatly can ever achieve greatly" and it's true that learning to fail well means breaking the program that tells us that "success is equal to right and therefore equal to good, while failure is equal to wrong and, as such, is bad." We have to learn to accept failure as a normal, healthy part of life. We all fail sometimes, and if we can learn to bend rather than break under the pressure of failure, we are much better off.

> "Only those who dare to fail greatly can ever achieve greatly."

Before he got the light bulb to work, Thomas Edison tried more than 2,000 experiments and combinations that failed. A young reporter asked him how it felt to fail so many times. He said, "I never failed once. I invented the light bulb. It just happened to be a 2000-step process." [38]

CHAPTER 4 ▶▶▶

So, see your failure as a lesson. In *Innovation and Entrepreneurship: Practice and Principles* Peter Drucker notes that researchers in one of the early German polymer labs occasionally made the mistake of leaving a Bunsen burner lit over the weekend. Upon discovering this mistake on Monday mornings, the chemists simply discarded the overcooked results and went on with their day.

Ten years later, a chemist in a polymer lab at DuPont made the same mistake. However, rather than simply discarding the mistake, the DuPont chemist analysed the result. He discovered that the fibres had congealed, which provided the first step towards the invention of nylon. With similar attention to the minor failure in the German lab, the Germans may have dominated the market with a decade-long head start on the development and production of nylon.[39]

So, understand the benefits of failure. As Ralph Waldo Emerson said, "All life is an experiment. The more experiments you make the better." Each failure is an opportunity for growth. Even if a failure costs you financially, the educational benefits can far outweigh the losses.

Fight the fear of success

We've covered a fear of failure, but as crazy as it may seem, a fear of success often prevents many people from achieving their goals. It is often hard to believe that someone would be afraid of success, but there are many reasons why, including:

> "All life is an experiment. The more experiments you make the better."

- Success involves change. The greater the success, the greater the change and change is often terrifying.

- You may expect more of yourself. You have to change familiar and comfortable ways of being for the new.

- People will expect you to succeed again. There is a new pressure to perform to a level that was not there before.

- You question if you can do it again. You may wonder if the first victory was a fluke the next time you perform, and if you fail, people will say it was an accident.

- People will notice you. If you used to being a wall-flower, this will take some adjusting.

- Your time demands will change. You may have less time because maintaining new levels of performance bring new demands on your time.

- People's expectations of you will change.

- It's harder to stay at the top than to get there. It was tough succeeding, but repeating it is usually even harder.

> "As crazy as it may seem, a fear of success often prevents many people from achieving their goals."

- People might like you less if you're successful. You may leave former peers behind when you raise the bar.

- Being a success changes your self-image. People may have told you, covertly or overtly, that you don't deserve success. You at least know your place as one who is average.

CHAPTER 4 ▶▶▶

The heart of the matter is this: many of us claim we want success, but we sabotage ourselves in countless ways. We procrastinate. We talk and talk, we dream and scheme, we plot and plan, and yet we never actually get around to doing anything. We never quite finish anything. We set our target just a little bit lower than we should.

> **"Many of us stave off success because, deep down, we feel we're not worthy."**

As with the fear of failure, many of us stave off success because, deep down, we feel we're not worthy. Why? Again, it goes back to our childhoods. Many of us received mixed messages about success while growing up. On the one hand, we were urged to do our best, to do everything perfectly, to finish whatever we began. On the other hand, we subconsciously observed that Tall Poppies were cut down at the roots — people who were successful were constantly criticised. Perhaps those around us may have started projects and never finished them; perhaps a parent was continually nitpicking and pointing out why something wouldn't work.

The underlying message may have been that success was not "all it's cracked up to be", or worse, that you weren't deserving of success. Could a fear of success be holding you back?

Identifying and eliminating your fear of failure or success will help you to set yourself up for the success you deserve, but in doing so, you'll uncover an interesting paradox: the goal itself is irrelevant. The real personal gain is in the pursuit of success, not in actually obtaining it. As they say in the classics, it is not what you earn, it's what you learn. It's not what you 'get' by securing your target, it's who you become in the process that really matters.

Whether you make a million dollars or not is unimportant, although you may need to make that much to work that lesson out. It is the type of person you develop into that will provide you with your source of happiness.

I am not my fear

We often think if we're experiencing fear that something must be wrong. It couldn't be further from the truth. We need to listen to what the fear is really telling us. It is not telling us we are falling apart, or that we shouldn't go forward until we know exactly what's ahead. Instead, fear means we are having a natural reaction to change and growth, as we face the new and unknown.

> **"Fear is a natural reaction to change and growth as we face the new and unknown."**

Very few of the things we feel afraid of are actually happening to us while we are afraid — they are things we fear might happen to us in the future. When I'm standing back stage, with a thousand people waiting for me to entertain and enlighten them, do I feel nervous? Hell, yes! But I ask myself: "what am I afraid of right now?" And it's always the fear of making a fool of myself, the fear of forgetting my train of thought, the fear of people not laughing at my jokes or not engaging with my presentation. And while I'm standing back stage, there's no way I can predict the outcome — whether I will make a fool of myself or not — so why feel afraid? When we are feeling fear we are usually not in the moment — which in this case is standing back stage with my colleagues. And when we are not in the moment, we are disconnected from our courage and our true self.

To pull yourself back into the moment, ask yourself "am I safe right now?" This will force you into present time and help you step back from your fear.

CHAPTER 4 ▸▸▸

Simply tell yourself:

I HAVE FEAR BUT I AM NOT MY FEAR

Dare to take a risk

In a world full of uncertainty, a fragile economy, and countless misfortunes that could happen to anyone, it's easy to see why most people are inclined to play it safe.

> "People who don't take risks generally make about two big mistakes a year. People who do take risks generally make about two big mistakes a year."

But playing it safe has its own inherent risks. If you never dare to fail your success will have a low ceiling. Most people underestimate their merit and ability to recover from failure, leading them to pass up valuable opportunities. The ability to fail big and fail often has been a mark of the spectacularly successful throughout history.

As Peter Drucker once said: "People who don't take risks generally make about two big mistakes a year. People who do take risks generally make about two big mistakes a year."

Most people are afraid of being broke and, as a result, are too conservative. The most critical thing about daring to risk is knowing that you can recover. Most people are ultra-conservative when it comes to personal exposure. So, the old chestnut about people being afraid to speak in public is true. When I stand in front of an audience and call for volunteers to come on stage, everyone will hide. But the problem with being risk averse is that we never get the chance to face and overcome our fears.

Many of us have some fear of speaking in public. In fact, the fear of public speaking or 'glossophobia' is believed to be the single most common phobia, affecting as much as 75 per cent of the population. Fear of public speaking consistently outranks fear of rats, snakes, spiders, dentists and heights. As Jerry Seinfeld observes, "the average person at a funeral would rather be in the casket than doing the eulogy."

When you ask someone who is afraid of speaking in public if they are interested in overcoming that fear, many times they'll ask why they need to bother. "I don't need to speak in public, so why bother overcoming the fear?"

> "The average person at a funeral would rather be in the casket than doing the eulogy."

Sure. They're right; they don't need to speak in public. But that's not the problem. The problem is they don't want to, and they're just saving themselves some embarrassment. Of course this embarrassment is imagined. It's not real.

To really break out of your self-limiting belief, you need to step out on stage and face your fear. It is easy to rationalise, to justify and to tell yourself: "I don't need to speak on stage". That may be true. However, there are probably also a host of other things you can't do either — things that would expand your sense of the world's possibilities. What could they be? Perhaps it's asking your potential soul mate out on a date; perhaps it's daring to quit your job, start a business, start a family or move to a new city.

Could it be that many wonderful opportunities remain impossible simply because you're not doing the things to move yourself forward?

The average person is driven by the need to be comfortable. In the drive to find comfort, we make ourselves more and more comfortable, which in turn

CHAPTER 4 ▸▸▸

leads to less and less risks. Less risk in turn means less and less growth — and the end result is we're petrified.

This solidification takes place over a long period of time. Most people don't see it happen. But speak to somebody in their mid 30s or 40s and you'll find that, most likely, they aren't doing much to break out of their comfort zone. Risk aversion imprisons them. And with each passing year, as they become more comfortable, they become less able to embrace change.

Change is the only constant in the universe. Just the other day, I heard a 40-year-old say "Oh, these youngsters with their knowledge of the Internet." He said, "It's too late for us." And there I am, aged 56, marvelling at his narrow perspective. I may not be a Gen Y whiz kid, but I'm determined to remain open to the possibilities the world offers us.

When you're weighing up the risks, consider the cost of missed opportunities. The biggest risk that people fail to consider is the benefit they lose by avoiding high risk/high reward opportunities. Without taking a risk, you can't exploit any opportunities that come your way. You can live a peaceful and reasonably happy life, but you are unlikely to create something new, and you are unlikely to make your mark on the world.

> "You'll miss 100 per cent of the shots you don't take."

If minimising risk is your modus operandi – don't expect outstanding results.

In business, as in just about every other endeavour from sport to romance, it's important to remember that you'll miss 100 per cent of the shots you don't take. Michael Jordan knew this. "There was never any fear for me, no fear of failure," he said. "If I miss a shot, so what?"[40]

Ask yourself: what if I chase my dreams and fall flat on my face? What is the worst that can possibly happen? How long will it take me to recover? The answer is probably less than you expect.

Now ask yourself this: how will I feel at the end of my life if I've let some nagging fears prevent me from reaching my full potential?

CHAPTER 4 ▸▸▸

Things to think about...

- As we grow and face change, it is inevitable that we experience some fear. Remember, as Nelson Mandela said, courage is not the absence of fear, but the triumph over it.

- Ask yourself: what fear could be stopping me from the success that I deserve?

- Recognise that the fear of failure hurts far more than the failure itself. Ask yourself: what if I set a target and I don't reach it? What is the worst thing that could happen?

- Only those who dare to fail greatly can ever achieve greatly. Learning to fail well is part of the secret to success. What positive lessons have you learnt in your life from your past failures?

- Many people have a real fear of success, because with success comes change. Could a fear of success be holding you back?

- When you are feeling fear, adopt this mantra: I have fear but I am not my fear.

- People who don't take risks generally make about two big mistakes a year. People who do take risks generally make about two big mistakes a year. Are you going to play it safe? Or are you going to dare to take a risk?

CHAPTER 5
Think abundance.

CHAPTER 5 ▶▶▶

If there's anyone who knows about the swings and roundabouts of making money, it's Donald Trump. The billionaire property developer owned towers, casinos, golf courses, hotel chains and even an airline before the effects of recession left Trump unable to meet his loan repayments in 1989. By 1991 Trump was facing business bankruptcy.

Ever wondered what it feels like to lose half of Manhattan? It didn't seem to faze The Donald, who embraced reality TV and bounced back with bigger and better projects. "Sometimes by losing a battle you find a new way to win the war," is his advice. And he's probably right: in its October 2007 list of billionaires Forbes valued Trump's wealth at $3.0 billion.[41]

While nothing on the scale of Trump's billion dollar losses, I've lost significant sums in my time. In 1988, Mary and I lost US$100,000 in a business venture that went bad. Now, I don't know what that sort of cash would be worth today, but let's just say, it was a significant amount of money for a modest, middle-class business couple like us. When I tell people the story — about how everyone advised me against it, but that I handed it over anyway and within six months there was nothing left and nothing to show for it — the obvious question is: "how did you handle that?"

> "Sometimes, by losing a battle you find a new way to win the war."

How did I handle it? Of course there was some grief and loss. There was shock and anger. And while it didn't happen immediately, within a few months I realised that the more I focused on "I've lost 100 grand", the more I was saying to myself "I can't earn it again."

Eventually, I was able to come to a point in my life where I could say, "I've gained a $100,000 worth of lessons out of the experience." I was able to use the experience as leverage in my next activity and a chance to do things differently next time around.

The same is very true for people going through a divorce and subsequent property settlement. Divorce is never pretty. When things are going well in life, we rarely say to ourselves "these coffee mugs are mine, but the kettle belongs to him." Our house is our house, our things are our things. People going through a property settlement usually come out the other side feeling like they've been torn apart. I've had clients say to me "I've split up with my wife and she's taken up with the bloke down the road, and now he's over at my place, watching my TV on my couch."

> "People going through a property settlement usually come out the other side feeling like they've been torn apart."

Nothing could be further from the truth. All of that stuff got split up during the property settlement. While he's resenting another man sitting on his couch, his ex-wife is sitting on it, wishing she could get rid of it because it reminds her of him.

I've got another client who was very smart. After suffering a devastating divorce, his $50 million business was dismantled to pay for the property settlement. He came out with a lot less than he thought he owned, but a year later met the woman who is now his wife. Together, they concluded that the remaining money from the previous relationship would hold them back from future happiness and success, so they decided to get rid of it.

They spent the best part of two years travelling the world, just spending money. They stayed at game parks in Africa, punted on the races in Hong Kong, enjoyed afternoon tea at the London Ritz. They had a fabulous time, and two years later they had nothing to show for it – except memories.

CHAPTER 5 ▸▸▸

Now, this man is very wealthy, because his wealth is between his ears. He has a very powerful abundance mentality and believes there's money to be made everywhere, and if he could make money once, he can do it again. And that's exactly what he's done. He and his new wife established a new business in a new industry in a new city and three years later are making $12 million a year. Meanwhile, his ex-wife is as poor as a church mouse. She's expended all her resources (clearly both her money and her ex-husband were valuable resources, and both are gone) and she has settled for a public service job and some 'security'.

> "Someone with an abundance mentality believes there is plenty out there for everyone."

And here we have a beautiful illustration of the difference between scarcity and abundance mentalities. Someone with an abundance mentality believes there is plenty out there for everyone. In contrast, someone with a scarcity mindset subconsciously believes there's only a finite amount of resources, and that they must protect their share.

In *The Seven Habits of Highly Effective People*, Stephen Covey says that most people are deeply scripted in the scarcity mentality. "They see life as having only so much, as though there were only one pie out there. And if someone were to get a big piece of the pie, it would mean less for everybody else. People with a scarcity mentality have a very difficult time sharing recognition and credit, power or profit..."[42]

Everyone knows someone with a firmly entrenched scarcity mentality. They penny pinch, they cut out coupons when they shop and they always look for the specials. And each time they engage in this limiting behaviour, it reaffirms their scarcity belief. "There isn't enough money so I better save every cent" is the outlook. As a result they continue to attract more limited thinking into their lives.

The scarcity mentality makes sense if you grew up during the Great Depression, when there was never enough to go around. But those who went through the depression didn't just pass on stories of hardship, they also passed on the idea that money was in short supply, along with the dominant mindset that "a penny saved is a penny earned", "money doesn't grow on trees", "save your pennies for a rainy day" and "a fool and his money are soon parted." When their children, the Baby Boomers, began to build the world we know today, they established businesses, practices and infrastructure that were naturally influenced by this way of thinking.

Where did that get us? Military spending is on the rise as our global leaders attempt to protect their precious patches of turf. A staggering US$1,339 billion dollars was spent on arms and other military expenditures in 2007, corresponding to 2.5 per cent of global gross domestic product and $202 for each of the world's 6.6 billion people. Not surprisingly, the United States spends by far the most on military arms, dishing out $547 billion last year, or 45 per cent of global expenditure. Britain, China, France and Japan — the next in line of big spenders — lag far behind, accounting for just four to five per cent of world military costs each.[43]

> "The poverty of our century is the result of a set of priorities imposed upon the rest of the world by the rich."

English Painter John Berger once said that "the poverty of our century is unlike that of any other. It is not, as poverty was before, the result of natural scarcity, but of a set of priorities imposed upon the rest of the world by the rich." Today we live in an age of material abundance, with free trade, open markets, stock and property booms, and the infinite riches of the information super-highway.

CHAPTER 5 ▶▶▶

And yet, our dominant world view is that the things we need to grow and prosper are in short supply. We're witnessing an ever-quickening pace of exploitation of energy, resources, land and habitat, as everyone becomes a competitor. Most of us walk around with a scarcity mentality that we'll lose something and never get it back. Each day is about survival, as there are not enough resources, projects, ventures, ideas and opportunities to go around.

The reason for this is simple: the fundamental concept of economics is scarcity. Values are set according to their relative scarcity. So, whether we're talking diamonds, gold, oil or coffee, their value is based on a real or perceived scarcity.

> "There is nothing abundant about plundering the natural and human resources of a bountiful planet in the fastest way possible."

The lack and need represented by this feeling of scarcity lies in a very human characteristic: greed. Advertising that encourages economic consumption (and economic growth) preys on a sense of scarcity within us. We are not complete or satisfied unless our houses are overflowing with designer homewares, gadgets and accessories, our wardrobes are teeming with designer fashions and our garage complete with a cool car. People find reassurance through consumption, even though the feeling of hunger can never be sated. But, as I've mentioned before, once we are trapped on the consumer treadmill, it's very hard to jump off.

Despite what the advertisers will have you believe, there is nothing abundant about plundering the natural and human resources of a bountiful planet in the fastest way possible. The industrialised world generates up to 730 kilograms of waste per person — that's every man, woman and child — each year. [44] This is the impact that excessive consumption has on our world.

It is a deep sense of insecurity, fear and scarcity thinking which leads to the grabbing and grasping of resources before they run out. And this way of acting becomes a self-fulfilling prophecy.

But what if the world isn't like that? What if there are plenty of resources for everyone? What if you were able to engage in a business environment that was more like a nurturing greenhouse than an arid desert?

Scarcity	Abundance
There isn't enough to go around	There's plenty out there for everyone
There's no room at the top	There's room for everyone to succeed
It's every man for himself	The sum is greater than all the parts
For every winner there is a loser	Winning is a win for everyone
There's never enough time	I take time for the things that matter
Ideas are hard to come by	There's never a shortage of new ideas
Look at all the resources we need	Look at all the resources we have
The market is full of threats	The market is full of opportunities
My competitors are taking my customers	There's plenty of business out there fore everyone
Win at all costs	Ensure that everyone wins
There's my way or the highway	There's my way, your way and a better way

So which is it? Is it a dog-eat-dog world? Or is it a place of opportunity for everyone who wants to have a go? You choose.

Think Win/Win

An abundance mentality helps you see that your success doesn't equal the failures of others. In *The Seven Habits of Highly Effective People*, Stephen Covey calls this a 'Win/Win' frame of mind.

CHAPTER 5 ▸▸▸

Win/Win sees life as a cooperative, not a competitive arena. Most people tend to think in terms of dichotomies: strong or weak, hardball or softball, win or lose. But that kind of thinking is fundamentally flawed. It's based on power and position rather than on principle. Win/Win is based on the paradigm that there is plenty for everybody, that one person's success is not achieved at the expense or exclusion of the success of others.[45]

A well known quote in sports tells us that "winning isn't everything; it's the only thing." Widely attributed to American football coach Vince Lombardi, the phrase captured the American public's attention during Lombardi's highly successful reign as coach of the Green Bay Packers in the 1960s. Over time, the quote adorned the walls of locker rooms, fired up pre-game pep talks and echoed from the rafters of banquet halls. But is winning really the only thing? Only if the other person wins too.

Have a look at the chart below, which outlines the six typical negotiation mindsets.

Mindset	Paradigm
Win/Win	The abundant paradigm: I win and you win.
Win/Lose	The competitive paradigm: if I win, you lose.
Lose/Win	The doormat paradigm: "alright, if it's important to you, then we'll do it your way."
Lose/Lose	The hypercompetitive paradigm: I want to see you lose, even if it means I lose too.
Win	The win at all costs paradigm: I am solely focused on getting what I want, regardless of the needs of others
Win/Win or no deal	The compromise paradigm: "Let's agree to disagree agreeably."

It's easy to see where the best results will come from. Anything other than a Win/Win solution means that someone loses. In most cases, 1 + 1 = 1.5, with time, energy and resources expended on arguing a point of view or position, competing, compromising or dividing up limited rewards.

While it may seem that winning is always better than losing, if you've ever won an argument at someone else's expense, you'll know that it's a hollow victory. (Johnathan Swift once said that "argument is the worst sort of conversation".) And if you've lost an argument yourself, you'll know that when you walk away from an argument with unmet needs, you feel resentment and bitterness, which sets up the potential for a Lose/Lose outcome in the future.

Here's a good example of this Win/Lose situation: a regular customer at a printer's has a reputation for being unpleasant, unreasonable and abusive. He constantly beats the price down on any negotiation, but does so in such a way that the business owner feels verbally abused. The customer may feel like he's getting a win, but the printer feels like he's losing. It is clearly a Win/Lose situation.

After several jobs, the printer begins to feel that the stress of working with this bloke is costing him more time, energy and grief than the jobs were worth. He begins to quote his jobs at twice the normal mark-up and refuses to budge on the price, changing the balance in this lopsided relationship. Of course, after a while, the client refuses to deal with customer, creating a Lose/Lose outcome in the long run.

> "Anything other than a Win/Win solution means that someone loses."

What about the compromise paradigm? Although regarded as a virtue, compromise ("you give a little, I'll give a little, and we'll meet each other half-

CHAPTER 5 ▸▸▸

way") has some serious drawbacks. Such bargaining often causes both sides to assume initial inflated positions, since they are aware that they are going to have to 'give a little' and want to buffer the loss (remember bartering in Bangkok markets or on the beach in Bali? The same principles apply). In addition, the compromise solution may be watered down or weakened to the point where it will not be effective. There may be little real commitment by anyone to the compromise.

> "It's not your way or my way; it's a better way, a higher way."

And of course, the competitive paradigm indicates a desire to meet one's own needs regardless of the needs of the others involved. The competitor uses some form of power, persuasion or coercion. Competitive strategies include the use of physical force (a punch in the nose, war); bribery (money, favours); and punishment (withholding love, money, job promotions). While the winner may feel their tactics have been successful, the real conflict may have only just begun. Losers may feel hostility, anxiety and physical damage as by-products of these Win/Lose power tactics. History is peppered with stories of wars that started with a Win/Lose.

The alternative is this: when everyone focuses their creative energy on finding the best outcome for everyone, the total reward can be: 1 + 1 = 3. As Covey says, "It's not your way or my way; it's a better way, a higher way." With a Win/Win mindset, all parties involved feel good about the solutions, agreements and decisions because everyone wins.

When you believe that there's plenty to go around, then the next step is to ask yourself: how can I work with my competitors? What can I learn from them?

In fact, the Latin root for the verb 'to compete' means 'to seek together' or 'to strive together'. Great people and great businesses don't worry about what they are losing from their competitors. They don't define themselves by competitive movements. Instead, they seek out new opportunities.

In the glory days of IBM, one of Thomas Watson's Golden Rules was "Thou shalt never badmouth a competitor". In fact, to violate this rule could result in instant dismissal. Tom Peters argues it makes good business sense to embrace the competition and to help others in your field succeed. "I think that when one badmouths one's competitors or tries to limit their activities, the 'word gets around'," he wrote on his blog in 2007. "And one develops a reputation as prickly and egocentric - and, well, as a selfish jerk."[46]

People with abundance mindsets really believe that the more they sell, the more there is to sell; the more they give, the more there is to give. Abundance thinkers believe there are only two kinds of people out there: those who are already customers and those who are waiting to become customers.

Case study:
The beauty of fair trade

People who think abundantly embrace the idea that the more successful they are, the more others are affected in a positive way.

Since Anita Roddick established her first store in Brighton, England, in 1976, The Body Shop has become a global empire of more than 2,000 stores in over 50 countries, making it the second largest cosmetic franchise in the world.

CHAPTER 5 ▸▸▸

One of the company's key competitive differentiators is its core values: against animal testing, support community trade, activate self-esteem, defend human rights and protect our planet.

The Body Shop's philosophy is not anti-capitalist or anti-globalisation. It is, in fact, in favour of international marketplaces. It uses its influence and profits for programs such as Trade Not Aid, aimed at promoting fair labour practices, safe working environments and pay equality.

The first fair trade partnership was established in the late 1980s, and by 1991, The Body Shop had started a paper factory in Nepal employing 37 people producing bags, notebooks and scented drawer liners, and a 3,000 square metre soap factory in a depressed Glasgow suburb, with 100 employees who had previously been chronically unemployed.

Today, 36 suppliers from 23 countries around the world — ranging from Nicaraguan sesame farmers to Indian handicraft producers — work in partnership with The Body Shop.

And everyone wins

- The Body Shop gets great ingredients and products; they also get to feel good about doing business with fairness, respect and trust.
- Suppliers benefit from fair pricing, and a sustained source of income which can be used for improving education or sanitation, building homes and modernising farming methods, to name but a few. They also gain access to markets and develop necessary business skills.
- Customers get high quality products and ingredients from around the world, and can feel good about spending their money with an ethical organisation.

> - Business is provided with a model of ethical trading and the opportunity to learn from The Body Shop's successes and failures and respond to the increasing demands for better standards of global trade.
>
> As Anita Roddick said: "Our trade with these communities is not just about creating another product or market for The Body Shop. It is about exchange and value, trade and respect, friendship and trust."[47]

Cultivating an abundance mentality

Today we tend to measure abundance in terms of the money and objects we possess. While our culture values those who earn, own and consume the most, the highest respect in Papua New Guinean tribal society is bestowed on those who give the most away.

And that's the bottom line: the fundamental concept of life on earth is abundance. The word 'abundance', from the Latin ab-unda, means 'overflowing'. Think water, bounty, plenty, a cornucopia of living things: trees, plants, animals, flowers. Scarcity thinking is linked to fear and unfulfilled needs; abundance is a sense of plenty in life, a sense of the bounty of living.

> Life itself, in a spiritual sense, is a continuous giving without thought of return. The sun is burning itself out without thought or sense of return. Plant life is ceaselessly growing, giving of its bounty without thought or sense of return. And we, as human beings, are gifts without return...[48]

CHAPTER 5 ▸▸▸

The world's artists understand this better than anyone. Goethe once said: "he who is plenteously provided for from within, needs but little from without." And what are many of the poems, paintings and plays of the world's great artists but a celebration of abundance?

So, abundance is the feeling of having plenty, with some to spare. But, does a man with millions in the bank, but whose mood fluctuates with the stock market, experience abundance? What about the people of the Amazon jungle, who have the bounty of the rainforest before them? Clearly, abundance is a state of mind.

In business, as in life, the scarcity mentality is limiting. It may seem like a good plan at first, but over time too much energy is wasted on conflict, negative thinking and stifled creativity. If you treat everyone around you like they're out to get you, they most likely will be. If you treat knowledge as a finite resource, you'll meet other people with the "I could tell you, but then I'd have to kill you" attitude. If you go into a project treating it like a neverending struggle for scarce resources that you must fight everyone else for, well guess what? It will probably turn out that way.

> **"Abundance is the feeling of having plenty, with some to spare."**

But if you trust that there is enough success to go around; if you believe that others don't need to fail in order for you to succeed; if you believe that life provides an abundance of opportunities, experiences and blessings, then one thing's for sure: you'll live a happier life, if nothing else. And you may just achieve some success along the way.

It's simply a matter of others reacting to your choices and actions. When you believe that the world is a good place, and that people are trustworthy, you're open and relaxed. You're more likely to notice and take advantage of any new contacts, lucky breaks or serendipitous events that come along. You're also more fun to be around, which means that you meet lots more positive, happy people who want to help you on your journey.

An abundance mentality flows from a deep sense of personal worth and security. It's more than simply having a positive attitude, although optimism is very important. People with abundance mentalities look at how things can be done, rather than why they can't be done. If you don't think abundantly already, affirm to yourself that there is an abundance of wealth, ideas and opportunities in the world. Abundance starts in your mind. The more you think abundantly, the more abundance you can enjoy. The more abundance you enjoy, the more success you will enjoy. Remember, the aim of the game isn't to take away a piece of someone's pie, it's to bake a whole new pie.

An abundance mentality is critical to business success. If you have trouble sustaining it, you aren't looking around you. While you stood in front of your wardrobe this morning wondering what you would wear today half the world's population was wondering where the next meal would come from.

> "An abundance mentality flows from a deep sense of personal worth and security."

Consider the story of a man who leaves the remote peasant village of his birth to travel the world. After many years, he returns home. His friends and family gather around him and ask: "How is life in the world?" He replies: "It is the same as here. It is good for those who know how to live."

CHAPTER 5 ▸▸▸

The art of abundance is not about getting rich quick, balancing your bank balance, thinking your way to riches or climbing the corporate ladder. It's about learning how to live.

Things to think about...

- If you lost everything, would you have the courage to start again? Would you have a choice not to?

- Do you have an abundance mentality or a scarcity mentality? Do you believe there is plenty out there for everyone? Or is there only a finite amount of resources, and must you do everything it takes to protect your share?

- What could abundance thinking do for your life? With an abundance of opportunities, what would be different in your professional life? What would be different in your personal life?

- Win/Win is based on the paradigm that there is plenty for everybody, and that one person's success does not mean someone else must fail. Remember: "It's not your way or my way; it's a better way, a higher way."

- Abundance is a state of mind, so learn to cultivate an abundance mentality. Affirm to yourself that there is an abundance of wealth, ideas and opportunities in the world.

CHAPTER 6
Surround yourself with success.

CHAPTER 6 ▶▶▶

The old cliché holds true: "It's not what you know, it's who you know." Most people really do get their jobs because of who they know.

The US Department of Labor, for instance, says that around 5 per cent of job seekers find their new position through the open market (advertisements online or in print publications). Another 24 per cent obtain jobs through contacting companies directly — the cold-contact method of job-hunting. Twenty-three per cent obtain jobs through employment agencies, college career-services offices and executive-search firms. The remaining 48 per cent — nearly half of all job hunters, obtain their jobs through referrals — that is, word of mouth.[49] How do they get referrals and find out about jobs through word of mouth? By networking.

For many people the word 'networking' conjures up schmoozing, boozing and using. For others, it seems like too much hard work. And for many, even the thought of chatting to a stranger about business is too daunting to contemplate.

> "If you're going to be successful in business, building a network of connections is vital."

But if you're going to be successful in business, building a network of connections is vital. And it's worth remembering that, while around 2 per cent of the population have no worries about walking into a room full of strangers and starting to chat, that leaves the remaining 98 per cent of the population feeling uncomfortable with the prospect of attending a function to network, introduce themselves to a stranger or develop new business contacts.

It's a small world after all

The small world phenomenon is an entrancing idea that the chain of social acquaintances required to connect one arbitrary person to another arbitrary person anywhere in the world is generally short.

The 'small world problem' takes its name from an experience familiar to us all. As psychologist Stanely Milgram describes it in his famous paper:

> Fred Jones of Peoria, sitting in a sidewalk cafe in Tunis, and needing a light for his cigarette, asks the man at the next table for a match. They fall into conversation; the stranger is an Englishman who, it turns out, spent several months in Detroit studying the operation of an interchangeable-bottlecap-factory. "I know it's a foolish question," says Jones, "but did you ever by any chance run into a fellow named Ben Arkadian? He's an old friend of mine, manages a chain of supermarkets in Detroit…"
>
> "Arkadian, Arkadian," the Englishman mutters. "Why, upon my soul, I believe I do! Small chap, very energetic, raised merry hell with the factory over a shipment of defective bottlecaps."
>
> "No kidding!" Jones exclaims in amazement.
>
> "Good lord, it's a small world, isn't it?"[50]

> **"Good lord, it's a small world, isn't it?"**

In 1967 Milgram asked a group of people, primarily from Omaha, Nebraska and Wichita, Kansas to reach a particular target person (usually in Boston)

CHAPTER 6 ▸▸▸

passing a message along a chain of acquaintances. When the person did not know the target, he or she was asked to think of a friend or relative who was more likely to know the target. They were then directed to record their name on a register and forward the packet to that person.

The results, originally published in 1967 in *Psychology Today*, found that of the 296 letters sent, 64 eventually reached the target contact, and among these chains, the average path length fell around 5.5 or 6. And, although Milgram himself never used the phrase "six degrees of separation", his findings helped coin the term that became part of popular culture.

The small world phenomenon eventually spawned a play, a movie and a game called Six Degrees of Kevin Bacon (in a nutshell, Bacon can be linked to any other actor in any movie that's ever been made — for example, he is connected to Marilyn Monroe by two steps because she was in The Misfits in 1961 with Eli Wallach. Bacon and Wallach performed together in Mystic River in 2003.[51])

> **"The average path length, or degree of separation, among the anonymised users was 6.6."**

Interestingly, Kevin Bacon cleverly capitalised on the game in his name to create a charitable social network to inspire giving to charities online. "SixDegrees.org is about using the idea that we are all connected to accomplish something good," said Bacon. "It is my hope that Six Degrees will soon be something more than a game or a gimmick. It will also be a force for good, by bringing a social conscience to social networking."

While the majority of chains in that study actually failed to complete, and some scientists questioned Milgram's methods, academic researchers continue to explore this phenomenon as Internet-based technology enhances the phone and postal systems only available during the times of Milgram. In June 2006, for instance, researchers from Microsoft and Carnegie Mellon University analysed 30 billion conversations among 240 million people using Microsoft Instant Messenger. They found that the average path length, or degree of separation, among the anonymised users was 6.6.[52]

What's more interesting than the "six degrees of separation" theory is Milgram's subsequent finding that some people received packages numerous time. In one experiment, 160 letters were mailed out with 24 reaching the target in his Sharon, Massachusetts home. Of those 24, 16 were given to the target person by the same person Milgram calls Mr Jacobs, a clothing merchant. Of those that reached him at his office, more than half came from two other men.[53]

> "There are people with a special gift for bringing the world together."

Building on this slice of research, Malcolm Gladwell, in The Tipping Point: *How Little Things Can Make a Big Difference*, examined how the six degrees theory could be dependent on a few extraordinary people, known as 'connectors' with large networks of contacts and friends. These connectors are essentially hubs that mediate the connections between the vast majority of otherwise weakly-connected individuals.

Of particular interest to us, Gladwell talks about the 'law of the few', in which "success of any kind of social epidemic is heavily dependent on the involvement of people with a particular and rare set of social skills."[54] Gladwell describes these people as mavens (or information specialists), salesman (charismatic people with powerful negotiation skills) and connectors - the people who "link us up with the world ... people with a special gift for bringing the world together." [55]

CHAPTER 6 ▸▸▸

American Playwright, John Gaure, ruminates upon this idea of connections in his 1990 play with the name — wait for it — Six Degrees of Separation. As one of the characters states:

> I read somewhere that everybody on this planet is separated by only six other people. Six degrees of separation between us and everyone else on this planet. The President of the United States, a gondolier in Venice, just fill in the names. I find it A) extremely comforting that we're so close, and B) like Chinese water torture that we're so close because you have to find the right six people to make the right connection... I am bound to everyone on this planet by a trail of six people." [56]

> "Every person you know could be a resource for an influential, life-changing contact with someone."

Everyone has a vast and powerful network. Each of us has anywhere from 250 to 3,000 contacts. If you know 250 people and each of those people knows 250 people, then at the second level of your network are 62,500 people!

Never underestimate the power of your contacts. Every person you know could be a resource for an influential, life-changing contact with someone. However, for some people the connections have become weak and rusty from neglect. Successful networks are built over a long period of time, not with the desperation of someone who needs the business tomorrow to stay afloat. Building a viable network is an ongoing process, not a one-time event. You have the choice and opportunity to have your network lead you to resources beyond your imagination.

What's the lesson in all of this? It's not what you know, but how connected you are.

Making the connections that count

The many manifestations of organisational change — from downsizing to outsourcing, and from merging to partnering, means that most companies are constantly redrawing their organisational charts. What's more, people in these companies are finding it less and less easy to find someone for support and advice, information and direction. This means people need to leverage their own personal networks to 'get the job done'.

> "The intensity and absolute necessity of networking has skyrocketed since we plummeted headlong into the Information Age."

In *It's Not What You Know, It's Who You Know: Work in the Information Age* Bonnie Nardi, Steve Whittaker and Heinrich Schwarz argue that "the intensity and absolute necessity of networking for practically everyone" has skyrocketed since we plummeted headlong into the Information Age.[57]

> In the not-so-distant past, much work took place in relatively stable settings. Many people were employed by large corporations. Long-term established relationships existed between businesses, suppliers, and customers. It was not unusual for white collar workers to stay at the same company for decades. Even blue collar workers subject to cycles of hiring and firing were often rehired by the same companies when economic conditions improved. Employees worked for long periods in 'communities of practice' in which they built up considerable expertise in the details of their job.[58]

CHAPTER 6 ▸▸▸

As tomorrow's businesses are built in cyberspace, and the working conditions of yesterday become obsolete, the old mentality of 'business is war' is no longer relevant. New kinds of alliances are being established between businesses, suppliers and customers. Connections outside the organisation, such as those with government and the media, are increasingly valuable. The low cost and real time transfer of ideas, knowledge and skills over the Internet has facilitated fast, fruitful collaboration. The Internet provides not only the communication channel, but the tool for people or businesses with niche interests to connect in the first place.

It is 'collabronauts' who, in seeking out new universes, will drive their businesses through the stratosphere. This idea of the 'collabronaut' was coined by Harvard Business School academic, Rosabeth Moss Kanter, who describes pioneers of the new global economy as "astronauts who explore outer space, explorers of cyberspace, explorers of new possibilities while creating links and connections, and explorers of the possibilities that can come through collaboration." [59]

In her book, *Evolve!: Succeeding in the Digital Culture of Tomorrow*, Kanter argues that the best collabronauts are skilled at making connections — both with people and ideas. They bring organisations closer together, create links, nurture relationships and initiate partnerships that may at first seem like uniting two groups from alien planets.

> **"The old mentality of 'business is war' is no longer relevant."**

Of course, competing organisations have been forming strategic partnerships and alliances for years, but the Internet facilitates a new breed of collaboration by connecting people to each other and opportunities that might not otherwise exist.

Think of it like this: a small strip mall with a bakery, a chemist, a grocer, a take-away pizza place and a DVD store may seem to be competing for customers, but in actual fact they are working together to draw customers to the mall. One customer buys bread while she is waiting for her medical scripts. Another orders a pizza and rents a DVD at the same time. Now big business is looking at doing this on a global scale.

It's not just the global empires that are recognising the importance of collaboration. Many small businesses are working alongside each other to produce a product, realise an idea, or develop a concept that can be sold in the global shopping mall that is the Internet. So, ask yourself this: what could the new era of collaboration do for my business?

Birds of a feather

Over the last fifty years or so, peer influence has emerged as the chief source of values and behavioural influence in adolescence, replacing the influence of adults. As teenagers seek to establish unique identities, away from the shadows of their parents, they form peer groups that help them define 'normal' in terms of attitude, thought and behaviour.

> "What could the new era of collaboration do for your business?"

Peer groups provide answers to questions and fears that parents are unable to resolve. They also provide the 'rules of life'. Wear these clothes, talk this way, act that way, and the group guarantees your acceptance. As a result, young people gain self-esteem from separating from parents and the group prospers as well. As each new member embraces the code, it verifies the correctness of that code to all the members.[60]

CHAPTER 6 ▸▸▸

The reason private schooling is becoming more popular is not because it provides a better education, but because it provides a more positive peer group. Parents are not buying an education; they are buying a peer group that will later become a powerful and influential network.

This social structure has a powerful effect on the way we interact with people throughout our lives. If we grab five of your friends and ask them about their net worth or average incomes, we are likely to predict yours.

People have always known this: that's why we say "birds of a feather flock together".

> **"The smart thing to do is to mix and mingle with people in the next success bracket to you."**

Look about you and you'll find that lawyers hang with other lawyers, artists with other artists and property developers with other property developers. If you want to become rich and successful, the best way to fast track that success is to surround yourself with rich and successful people.

The smart thing to do is to mix and mingle with people in the next success bracket to you. If you are a plumber, but have aspirations to become a property developer, then you need to find ways to seek out the people who have already achieved what you desire. Start to move in their orbit. You'll gain subtle and subconscious lessons and ideas that can radically alter your thinking and your results.

One of our recent breakthroughs has occurred because, after 25 years in business, Mary and I started to be influenced by people who thought and acted differently to us. They looked at our business and laughed, asking "why do you do that?" or "what is the point in this?" They wondered why we wanted to work so hard for so little reward, and came up with crazy ideas that we knew couldn't possibly work.

But with time, their influence started to have a profound effect on us. We started to listen. We learned. We applied some of those crazy ideas. And guess what? They worked.

What you'll find when socialising with people more successful than you is that, rather than having a superior product or business model, they have a superior method of thinking. And that thinking will rub off on you. It's called osmosis. You don't need to sit down and say: "tell me everything you know". They probably can't tell you that, even if they want to. But just in listening to their conversations, hearing about their challenges and successes, you'll start to gain know-how and knowledge in your chosen field.

> "Take it step by step, and learn from people a little bit further ahead on the road to success."

As you surround yourself with successful people, you'll find that they are delighted to pass their knowledge on to you. Why? When you give away bread, you lose bread. When you give away knowledge, you simply share it. In fact, you reinforce it, because you come to a better understanding of it yourself.

Don't feel embarrassed about the fact that you haven't made it yet. Make your moves in increments. You don't have to leap from laying bricks to schmoozing with the multimillionaires. An apprentice bricklayer needs to learn how to lay bricks before he can start building skyscrapers. You can take it step by step, learning from people a little bit further ahead on the road to success.

CHAPTER 6 ▶▶▶

Making the most of a mentor

A good mentor seems to have magical powers that can help you to transform your business. A good mentor has heard it all before, has said it all before, and has done it all before.

A good mentor is there to help you learn from their mistakes. As someone in the personal development field, I can tell you the reason I see the problems in other people's lives (and how to fix them) is simply because I'm not involved in them. I come to their lives and situations with fresh eyes; I'm not seeing through the muddied-up lens of the person living the dramas, which makes my insight into their problems and their solutions crystal clear.

> "A good mentor has magical powers that can help you to transform your business."

A mentor works in exactly the same way, by examining your business and asking you "why are you doing that?" He or she can objectively observe how you operate, provide you with a glimpse around a blind corner, or point out ways you could improve.

When I work with corporations on change management, leadership or team building, I always ask for a show of hands: "who has been here more than five years?" Each year, the number of people putting up their hands — across companies and industries — has dwindled. The organisational implications of this are profound: most companies are seeing 100 per cent turn over in a five year period. Not only is corporate knowledge lost, but many companies no longer have a collection of older, wiser workers to turn to for advice and assistance.

As I mentioned earlier, this shift from corporate to individual knowledge is placing a newfound emphasis on our own personal networks. It's also driving the coaching industry, as people in need of some objective advice need to seek it outside their organisations. And that's why they are working with mentors.

While I mentor many people myself, I have my own mentor who charges me $10,000 just to say hello. But, if I can a make a million dollars in a month simply because of this fellow's advice, is it worth ten grand to ring him up?

There's a mentor for people at every price point. I assume that the person coaching Bill Gates is being paid more than $100 an hour, and at the other end of the spectrum, some organisations, such as churches and charities, have volunteer mentors. Whatever your investment, there are a few things you should look for in a mentor.

> "Don't take advice from a financial advisor who hasn't made more money than you have."

To start with, it's worth employing a basic rule of thumb: don't take advice from a financial advisor who hasn't made more money than you have. If you want to be successful, seek out a mentor who is more successful than you. Old mentors are often better than young ones simply because they've been around for a long time, but that's not to say that a younger mentor might not suit you. The important thing is that they've succeeded in doing something that you haven't.

The next rule is to choose someone who has current knowledge. If you want to become an Internet entrepreneur, there's no point learning from someone who hung up her keyboard and mouse mat in the late '90s. A

CHAPTER 6 ▸▸▸

good mentor knows how to succeed in the current business environment. Our world is in such a state of flux, and things change so rapidly, that you don't want to be learning tips and techniques for selling real estate from someone who still thinks the median house price in Sydney is $200,000.

There's an almost guaranteed method for getting someone to coach you. Once you've identified that person I think the next step is to approach them and say, "How do I make it worthwhile for you to mentor me?" You want the person to know that there is going to be benefit in the exchange for them.

Knocking on their door and asking, "How many dollars would it take" is the least successful method of getting the help you desire. A really good mentor is not going to be looking at the prospect as a financial transaction, but more as a chance to pass on their knowledge and wisdom. They may not want to work with someone who simply wants to buy their knowledge, because that can be done with a book, CD set or workshop.

Mentoring is about establishing a relationship. You need to foster rapport, and there must be a fair and equitable exchange. For the mentor to give you all their knowledge and wisdom, what are they going to get in return? The easiest way to find out is to ask. You may find they want you to mow the lawns, do some community service, help them write a book. Whatever it is, the only way you'll find out is to ask.

Many of us fall into the trap of believing that we can do it all on our own. Expand your thinking beyond yourself — the "I can do it on my own" mentality limits your outreach and effectiveness in business. Many of us need to retrain ourselves to think positively about interdependence — about capitalising on the skills, knowledge, talent and resources of the people around us.

◄◄◄ SURROUND YOURSELF WITH SUCCESS

As Jack Welch, former Chairman and CEO of General Electric, once said "winning is about having the very best people. It doesn't help you if you're surrounded by people who are less talented than you are. You're lucky if your team mates are better and faster than you are, even if you are pretty good. And that's true in business, too. You can't win alone. You just can't." [61]

**Case study:
Keeping your head out of the clouds**

When music entrepreneur Richard Branson decided to start an airline called Virgin Atlantic, one of the first things he did was contact a man who had experience doing what he was trying to do.

This man was Sir Freddie Laker, an aviation pioneer who broke the monopoly in the skies when he introduced cheap air travel to the world in the 1970s. At its peak, Laker Airways offered London to New York tickets for £118, but was forced out of business in 1982 by a cartel of ten airlines that wanted to keep ticket prices painfully high.

Richard Branson later said "There was a lot to learn about starting Virgin Atlantic, so I asked Sir Freddie Laker whether he could help me."

Laker's experience and expertise helped Branson to compete with British Airways as Branson built on Laker's concept of radically cheaper tickets, austere cabins and passengers paying for their food.

CHAPTER 6 ▸▸▸

Freddie Laker died in 2006, and in remembering his mentor, Richard Branson wrote: "I got to know Freddie Laker very well... I wanted to name our first plane after him, but he insisted it wouldn't be good for our image as a new start-up. It would be years before he let us christen a Jumbo 'Spirit of Sir Freddie'. He also gave me fantastic advice about Virgin Atlantic. He warned me I would have to defend my business against monopolist and protectionist governments, and also explained why we needed to beat competitors on quality of service as well as price.

He concluded his advice with the immortal words: "When BA come after you, which they inevitably will, shout long, shout hard and then sue the bastards!" Branson said that "within six years everything he had predicted in that one sentence came true, but — partly thanks to his advice — we won."

Laker's generosity of spirit paid off for Branson and Virgin Atlantic. According to the airline's annual report, Virgin Atlantic carried around 5.1 million passengers and made an annual profit of £46.8 million in 2007.

Things to think about…

- It's not what you know, but who you know. Never underestimate the power of your contacts. Every person you know could be a resource for an influential, life-changing contact.

- What steps are you going to take to make sure you surround yourself with the people who can take your life to the next level?

- Think collaboratively. Who could you work with to produce a product, deliver a service or develop a concept? Who could you partner with on the road to success?

- Birds of a feather really do flock together. So, seek out people in the next success bracket to you and learn the secrets of success from the people who've been there and done that.

- Find yourself a mentor. No one can do it alone — not even you! Find someone who can help you with support, advice and the occasional prod when you need it!

CHAPTER 7
Leverage yourself.

CHAPTER 7 ▶▶▶

In *The Millionaire Next Door*, one of the millionaires interviewed shared a wonderful anecdote about his wealth philosophy. "My family in Nebraska understood the value of a dollar," this independently wealthy man told the researchers.

"Dad used to say seeds are a lot like dollars. You can eat the seeds or sow them. But when you would see what seeds turned into — ten-foot-high corn — you don't want to waste them. Consume them or plant them. I always get a kick out of watching things grow."[62]

> "In business, leverage means increasing your power of advantage."

This man knew the power of leverage. Start with something small, nurture it, watch it grow, reinvest, renew, see more growth... the power of leverage was right there before his eyes.

In physics, leverage is a factor by which a lever multiplies a force. In business, it means increasing your power of advantage.

So, how do you gain leverage? In this chapter, I'm going to look at three things you can leverage to be successful: your time, your knowledge, and the knowledge of others.

Recovery from the entrepreneurial seizure

In his seminal work, The *E-Myth*, Michael Gerber says that most people have an 'entrepreneurial moment', where they are, for a fleeting second in time "suddenly stricken with an Entrepreneurial Seizure."[63]

One day, after years of doing technical work (whether as a carpenter, mechanic, hairdresser, bookkeeper, computer programmer, doctor, plumber or salesperson) we have a sudden flash, where we ask ourselves: "Why am I working for this guy when I could be doing it for myself?"

> "Most business people are suddenly stricken with an Entrepreneurial Seizure."

Once the idea of being our own boss takes hold, most of us dive deep into the adventure of small business without really ever thinking beyond the basics.

Mary and I certainly had that entrepreneurial attack, back in May 1984, which resulted in us starting our own business. As I've mentioned previously, we had a fair degree of success, particularly in the early days, when personal growth was a boom industry and people couldn't sign up for our courses fast enough.

There was one fatal flaw in our business strategy, though. Our Achilles Heel was that our business was entirely dependent on us working in it. If we wanted extra cash, we put on another seminar. If we wanted to work less, our bottom line suffered. Any business analyst would have seen in an instant what it took us 25 years to see: that we didn't have a business, we had a promotion. We had no way to replicate our business, because it was reliant on me delivering the product. And our business would be fine provided I continued to promote and deliver. But what happened if something happened to me?

The not-so-obvious downside to 'just run another workshop' is that, like you, I have an uncanny ability to spend all the money I earn. Since I was constantly running out of money and solving the problem with working

CHAPTER 7 ▸▸▸

longer hours — I quickly fell into the old trap of the business owning me rather than the other way around.

A friend a mine once said to me, "Paul, we started our business because we had a vision that it could do more for us; that it would provide more for our kids and our family. We believed we'd have a better quality of life."

"Little did I know," she said, "that we were creating a monster that demanded to be fed every day. It is running on the fuel that we supply it every day. As long as we continue to supply that fuel, it will continue to demand it."

> **"Most traditional business owners all say the same thing: their success is limited by the number of hours they work."**

What we don't think about is how to make ourselves redundant. It's always the last question business owners ask themselves. But it should be the first.

If you are the key person in your business, without you, the business won't run. If this fits your business, then you're not alone. Most traditional business owners all say the same thing: their success is limited by the number of hours they work.

We need a seismic shift in thinking to take ourselves out of the day-to-day running of the business.

Let's say, for example, that your business makes $60,000 a year. You can pay someone $50,000 a year to do most of the day-to-day tasks that overburden you, leaving you to concentrate on the strategic tasks of moving the business forward. While your average business owner would see this as a cost of $50,000 to the business, what you need to see is that by paying someone to do your job, you are now making $10,000 a year for doing nothing. And you now have the space to reproduce your efforts. Again. And again. And again.

How often do you need to do that? As many times as it takes to gain financial independence. As Michael Gerber suggests, "go to work on your business as if it were the pre-production prototype of a mass-producible product." [64]

> "Go to work on your business as if it were the pre-production prototype of a mass-producible product."

Leverage your time

Imagine that you built a website, which sold a widget. Imagine the cost of buying the widget and delivering it was less than the cost to maintain the website. Now, imagine the website made $100 a week. In this scenario, you've got all your expenses covered and you're making $100 each week in profit.

Under those circumstances, wouldn't you start thinking: "I can buy another widget and set up another website and make another $100 a week"?

Logically, the answer is yes, of course you would do this. It's the smart fisherman's principle: while one line in the water limits the number of fish he can catch, an astute angler knows if he puts ten lines with ten different baits into the water at the same time, his fish-catching potential will rise.

Let's look at it from another point of view. In *The E-Myth Revisited*, Michael Gerber points to the success of McDonald's. Whether you like their hamburgers or not, you have to admit the McDonald's phenomenon has been incredible.

CHAPTER 7 ▶ ▶ ▶

According to Gerber, McDonald's creator, Ray Kroc, was "forced to create a business that worked in order to sell it, he also created a business that would work once it was sold, no matter who bought it."[65]

He developed a foolproof, predictable business that was systems-dependent, not people-dependent.

Today, McDonald's is the leading global food service retailer with more than 30,000 local restaurants serving 52 million people in more than 100 countries each day. In 2007, McDonald's sold $5.7 billion dollars worth of hamburgers worldwide! [66]

The most exciting part of the McDonald's story for me is that I have yet to find anyone who says that a Big Mac is the best burger they have ever tasted. It's proof that the system is more important than the product.

Unlike most small business owners before him — and since — Ray Kroc went to work on his business, not in it.[67] I'm going to cover this concept in a later chapter, but for now, what can the McDonald's model teach us about building a business that works without you?

> "Develop a foolproof, predictable business that is systems-dependent, not people-dependent."

If you have a McDonald's store and it made you some money, would you go get another one? Chances are you would. It just makes sense that you'd get another one. And another one. And another one. In fact, that's the McDonald's model: many McDonald's franchisees own more than one restaurant.

Why? Because they don't have to work in them.

So, the thing that separates a McDonalds system from others is that the owner is redundant. The income is passive and you can get on with finding the next big thing.

I'm not suggesting everyone rush out and buy a McDonald's franchise. And I'm not suggesting that purchasing a McDonald's will give you the challenge, excitement and self-satisfaction that you may be looking for. But purely from an analytical point of view, if one of these things makes you some money, then two of them would make double. Three would make triple. Right? Assuming you can find the capital, why wouldn't you do it?

What I'm suggesting is that we need to think strategically about multiple strands of income.

The question is this: "how many different ways can I attract income into my personal orbit?" And then, "how do I make them passive streams?"

Michael Gerber says the McDonald's model is successful for three reasons, because it:

1. Exceeds the expectations of customers, employees, partners;
2. Is structured and systems-dependent, and so doesn't rely on employee expertise; and
3. Provides a uniformly predictable service to the customer.

The bottom line is that most people don't enter their business — whether butcher, baker or candlestick maker — thinking that they'll franchise it.

But why can't you?

CHAPTER 7 ▸▸▸

> "What we have to leverage is our know-how."

Leverage your knowledge

Seventeenth century 'thought leader', Francis Bacon, got it right when he famously said that knowledge is power. Today's global economy is an information society where know-how, expertise and intellectual property are even more critical than other economic resources such as land, oil or even human labour.

Peter Drucker first introduced the concept of the knowledge economy in 1996, when his book *The Effective Executive* described the distinctions between the manual worker and the knowledge worker. A manual worker works with his or her hands to produce 'stuff' while a knowledge worker produces ideas, knowledge or information — essentially something you can't drop on your foot.[68]

Corporations around the globe realise that knowledge is the key to business growth and success. "We can no longer compete on the cost of labour with countries like China," Carlo de Benedetti, chief executive of Italy's Olivetti, told the Wall Street Journal Europe. "What we have to leverage is our know-how." [69] Or, as Tom Peters says, what we need is "more intellect, less materials".[70]

The most important thing about knowledge is that it has no upper limit. Unlike capital, labour, resources and other measures of the industrial age, knowledge doesn't deplete with use. According to high technology analysts, IDC, 161 billion gigabytes of knowledge was created in 2006. That's three million times the information in every book ever written. In the next three years the digital universe is expected to expand six fold.[71]

If, as Peters suggests, the "only asset is the human imagination" and that knowledge is the primary basis for value-adding in today's companies, what can you do to capitalise on your knowledge? [72]

In *Getting Everything You Can Out of All You've Got*, Jay Abraham pinpoints three questions that he says can change your life. They are:

1. Have you identified and valued your true expertise and inventoried your negotiable personal assets?
2. What performance skills have you demonstrated in the past that have not only abstract, but intrinsic, value and importance to a business — or a specific type of business?
3. What have you accomplished that people would not only respect, but also desire to learn and utilise to gain the same benefits for their companies? [73]

> "The only asset is the human imagination."

The Internet revolution is leading to a twenty-first century renaissance of ideas and innovation. And whether you're living in New York or Newcastle, Venice or Vientiane, you have the same access to the sum of all human knowledge on the information superhighway.

With geographical isolation and the tyranny of distance now a memory, the world has become 'flat' and anything that can be done, will be done. The only question is: will it be done by you or to you?

CHAPTER 7 ▶ ▶ ▶

Most people don't realise that the skills they gain from running a delicatessen will help them when they move onto something grander. In 18 months of slicing ham and balancing the books at the deli, you broaden your knowledge of business and managing people. Not to mention that, you'll probably gain skills that will make you a better partner or parent.

Have you ever thought that maybe those 20 years as a nurse are the very thing that will equip you with the knowledge you need for your next challenge in life? As we move through life, we gather momentum based on this expanding knowledge and practical experience. That's why you see people hit their fifties and become extraordinarily productive.

> "As we move through life, we gather momentum based on our expanding knowledge and practical experience."

I took a call recently from a client who was wondering whether, at 61 years of age, he was too old to open up his own real estate agency business. Despite being the number one sales person in a large national agency, he was having a crisis of faith.

"I think you're probably at the best point in your life," I told him. Surprised, he asked why.

"Everything you've learned so far is going to help you, I explained. "You just need to learn a few things about running a business instead of working in one. But aside from that, many of the big questions in your life have been answered."

What did I mean, he wondered.

"You're kids have grown up and the great question about whether you were a good father has already been answered. You either did a good job or you didn't, but the question has been resolved. Likewise, the questions about whether you were a good husband or provider have been pretty much answered, and all the energy that would be diverted to those is free for you to concentrate on your business."

The idea was revolutionary to him.

In fact, it is a rallying cry for all those Baby Boomers and their sea changes, tree changes or other life changes that involve downsizing, part timing or retiring from the workforce.

We're living longer than ever before, we're healthier and wealthier and people in their 50s and even 60s are probably now at the peak of their productivity. Our culture has failed to grasp this opportunity yet. But the ground is beginning to shift underneath us, and as the pool of available workers dwindles, as libraries and universities lose their status as the sole repositories of knowledge, the lifetime of skills and knowledge of Baby Boomers is needed more than ever.

> "The lifetime of skills and knowledge of Baby Boomers is needed more than ever."

The oldest non-Nepalese to climb Mount Everest was seventy. In 2003, Yuichiro Miura, a professional skier and a high school headmaster from Sapporo in Japan became the oldest man to reach the summit of Mount Everest at the age of 70.[74] With that in mind, how long ago was 65 considered well past your prime?

CHAPTER 7 ▶▶▶

We've all heard the story about Roger Bannister breaking the four-minute mile barrier in 1954. Prior to his breakthrough, it was thought be humanly impossible to run a mile in under four minutes, and yet the record has been smashed since by many athletes, and lowered by almost 17 seconds in the last 50 years. In 1994 Eamonn Coghlan became the first and, as of April 2008, only man over the age 40 to run a sub-four minute mile on the Harvard University indoor track. He was 41 at the time.[75]

So, we need to ask ourselves, is 40 over the hill? Is 50? Is 60? As a 56-year-old, I look at the things that I want to do physically and they're the things that previously were considered the domain of 30 year olds.

> "The human brain continues to grow and increase in intelligence throughout a person's life."

We can be active and productive in our 80s and 90s. Many Baby Boomers will choose never to retire, not because they can't afford to (although it's true that many can't), but because they can't handle the boredom. They want to be actively engaged in life, challenge and experience.

We know now that the human brain continues to grow and increase in intelligence throughout a person's life. In 1947, every single child in Scotland took the same exam to test their intelligence quotient (IQ). Sixty years on, researchers at the University of Edinburgh tracked down one thousand of the original participants, who are now in their 70s, to have their brain function measured again to compare it with the results from six decades ago. They also underwent brain scans and genetic tests, along with answering health and lifestyle questionnaires, to determine factors that impact on mental ability.

From this, researchers were able to determine that the way you live can raise or lower your cognitive skills by around 10 per cent. Factors such as smoking, poor diet and physical fitness had an impact on someone's IQ level at 70, but so did working in a stimulating job. In fact, people who had used their brains the most often showed a slight increase in IQ. In other words, what you don't use, you lose, but what you do use can magnify.[76]

Those indicators — smoking, diet and fitness — are not traditionally noted as business success ingredients.

Trust me.

They are.

What's happened to your ability with mental arithmetic since calculators became commonplace? If you're like most people, you'll admit that while once you could calculate long division in your head, now you need help with your times tables. It's the same with phone numbers. How many people can't remember even their own phone number now that their directory is programmed into their phone? When you don't have to remember, you don't. It's that simple.

> "What you don't use, you lose, both physically and mentally."

There's a parallel to be made here between the mind and the body. What you don't use, you lose, both physically and mentally. If you exercise your body and feed it healthy food, chances are it's going to last longer and you'll be capable of doing more. Strap your arm to your body for three weeks and then undo the strap. See how hard it is to pick up your cup of tea.

CHAPTER 7 ▶▶▶

So, challenge your brain. Challenge yourself. Just as you need to keep adjusting your weight regime at the gym to keep challenging your body, you need to do the same with your brain — up the intensity, adjust the exercise.

Leverage others' knowledge

When you borrow money from the bank to buy a house, you're leveraging other people's money. Most of us get that idea of leverage. But we don't embrace the concept of leveraging other people's knowledge. When you run into legal trouble, the first port of call is your lawyer. When balancing the books becomes tricky, you see your accountant. When you get sick, off to the doctor you trot. In all of these cases, you are simply leveraging another person's knowledge for your own benefit.

> **"You can't know it all. There is simply no way to acquire all the wisdom you need to make your business thrive."**

We are all comfortable with the idea of leveraging people's labour. Many people have determined that, if they are earning $40 an hour, paying someone $20 an hour to clean the house makes smart business sense. That way, you can have two things happen at once — you can have the house cleaned and earn money.

So, why wouldn't you leverage someone's knowledge about marketing to help you boost your business? Why not leverage someone's years of research into demographics to pinpoint the best target market for your business? Why not tap into someone's creative ideas to help you spur on your own dreams.

"You can't know it all," advises property developer, Donald Trump. "No matter how smart you are, no matter how comprehensive your education, no matter how wide ranging your experience, there is simply no way to acquire all the wisdom you need to make your business thrive."[77]

Say you want to become the next Donald Trump. The quickest way to learn how to become a property developer is to hang around people who've been doing it. There are plenty of people who will tell you what you want to know. And if you can't find anyone who'll share some knowledge in person, there are plenty of books and workshops and seminars and DVDs that could help you too. So, why wouldn't you do it?

No one becomes an overnight success story. No one goes from laying bricks to owning a multi-million dollar property empire overnight.

Instead, it's more likely to happen like this. Imagine you're a bricklayer and you're good at what you do. With a reputation for excellence, you need some help to cover all the work required of you. So, you hire an apprentice. And you complain about how the apprentice slows you down while you teach him how to lay bricks. And you wonder whether it's worth the hassle. But you persist, and soon the apprentice starts to contribute to the speed of your brick laying; instead of laying 1,000 bricks a day, you're putting down 1,100, then 1,200, then 1,500. As things keep on progressing, the apprentice becomes more confident and skilled, and soon you're laying 2,000 bricks a day.

> "No one becomes an overnight success story."

CHAPTER 7 ▶▶▶

You've doubled your efforts, and it gives you time to start talking to developers about opportunities for your business. You spend a day a week out in the field, which changes your job role from 100 per cent brick layer, to 80/20 brickie and salesman. There are some inevitable challenges of the new job role, but as you progress, you need more people. You take on another apprentice. And another. You hire some qualified tradesmen to oversee them.

> **"Successful business people understand that learning is a lifetime occupation."**

You build up the business to the point where you're not laying any bricks at all. Despite this, 5,000 bricks are being laid by your business everyday. You're out rubbing shoulders with developers, and learning to speak their language, gaining the know-how and gleaning knowledge about the ins and outs of developing property in your market. Then, one day you're told about a small development opportunity that's been overlooked. In fact, one of your contacts suggests it's a great investment, but he doesn't have the time or resources to fit it into his workload.

You take a risk, borrow money to purchase the land, and put a house on it. Of course the bricks get laid cheaply, and you call in some favours for the electrics and plumbing. The result? A small profit. Now, are you a bricklayer or a developer? And what did you learn?

At this point, most of us would say: "you beauty, I'm going to upgrade the truck and splurge on a flat screen TV. I deserve it. I've worked hard." But would that be the smart thing to do? Imagine, instead, that you recognise you are at the same point you were when you hired your apprentice. And so you buy two blocks of land and build two houses. During the process, you learn more, and you meet more people who are doing the same thing as you, just on a grander scale. You ask questions, learn some tips and tricks, and on you go to greater and greater success. You've made the radical paradigm shift from thinking like a wage earner to thinking like an entrepreneur.

Here's where the twenty-year overnight success comes in. In the example above, you'll make more money in the most recent year than in all the years before it combined.

Successful business people understand that learning is a lifetime occupation. Not only is the reservoir of knowledge so vast, but it is ever increasing. The average person today receives more information on a daily basis than the average person received in a lifetime in 1900.[78] The average Australian worker receives hundreds of messages (email, phone, snail mail or SMS) per day. Half of what is known today, we did not know ten years ago.[79] The amount of knowledge in the world has doubled in the last ten years. And, according to Moore's Law, it is doubling again every two years.[80]

> "You receive more information on a daily basis than the average person received in a lifetime in 1900."

To keep up with this rate of change, you must be on a path of continual improvement. Many of us fall into the trap of thinking our mental development ends when we complete our formal education. As soon as we leave the external discipline of school, we let our minds atrophy. We don't commit ourselves to reading, we don't explore new subjects in any depth, we don't write down our thoughts or critically analyse the way we see the world. Instead, we spend our time watching TV.

CHAPTER 7 ▸▸▸

A recent survey indicated that Australians spend 47 hours each week watching television, playing computer games and surfing the Internet.[81] That's more than a full-time job! While some television has value, and certainly the Internet is a fantastic resource, if you're serious about business success, you need to get serious about how you use your time. Rather than watching TV, wasting hours on Facebook or playing World of Warcraft, you could immerse yourself in relevant business books, study the art of negotiation or leadership, or write a journal to explore your own thoughts, insights and learnings. You could spend your time socialising with people who can help you climb the ladder of success, or with a mentor who offers that one million dollar suggestion.

Successful business people know that knowledge does not just come from external sources. William Shakespeare suggested that "learning is but an adjunct to ourselves" — in other words, seek knowledge from within. Think of yourself as a multi-dimensional entity of resources and contacts. Who you are consists of all of your life experiences and the people who influence who you are as a person. You are larger than what you see in your mirror. You are a culmination of connections that provide an unlimited source of knowledge and opportunities.

> "Learning is but an adjunct to ourselves, so seek knowledge from within."

The last word on leverage

A lever is a device that multiplies the effort applied. Archimedes once said: "If I had a lever long enough I could move the world". The concept applies to better output: if we apply enough leverage we can achieve better results. Successful business people don't think in terms of saving time, they think of leveraging time. An even more precious asset — knowledge — can also be leveraged. As Jay Abrahams advises, "think: highest and best use of your time, money, and effort. Highest and best. Always highest and best!"[82]

**Case study:
The first red millionaire**

One eighth of the world's population has laid hands on 'The Cube', the most popular puzzle in history and the colourful brainchild of Erno Rubik.

Twenty-nine year old Hungarian Rubik was not initially interested in producing a toy. He was concerned with the structural design problem the cube presented, asking himself "how could the blocks move independently without falling apart?"

Rubik applied for his Hungarian patent in January 1975 and left his invention with a small toy making cooperative in Budapest. The patent approval finally came in early 1977 and the first Cube appeared at the end of 1977.

Sales of the Rubik's Cube were sluggish until Hungarian businessman Tibor Laczi discovered the Cube. While having a coffee, he spied a waiter playing with the toy. The next day Laczi went to the state trading company, Konsumex, and asked permission to sell the Cube in the West.

CHAPTER 7 ▶▶▶

"When Rubik first walked into the room I felt like giving him some money," Laczi said. "He looked like a beggar. He was terribly dressed, and he had a cheap Hungarian cigarette hanging out of his mouth. But I knew I had a genius on my hands. I told him we could sell millions."

They certainly did sell millions and Erno Rubik became the first self-made millionaire from the communist block. Between 1980 and 1982, more than 100 million Rubik's Cubes were sold worldwide.[83]

Things to think about…

- Leverage means increasing your power of advantage. Ask yourself: how can I gain leverage in my life?

- Whether you're a butcher, a baker or a candlestick maker, you must think about how you will franchise your business. How are you going to work on your business as if it were the pre-production prototype of a mass-producible product?

- Leverage your time. Look for opportunities just like McDonald's – those that aren't dependent on your time. Ask yourself: how will I make myself redundant?

- Ask yourself: how many different ways can I attract income into my personal orbit? How do I make them passive streams?

- The only asset is the human imagination and knowledge is the primary basis for value-adding in today's world. What can you do to capitalise on your knowledge?

- When you don't use it, you lose it. So challenge your brain and challenge yourself. Up the intensity, adjust the exercise.

CHAPTER 7 ▸▸▸

Things to think about...cont

- Leverage others' knowledge. Who has knowledge that could benefit you? Who has creativity, experience or a rich understanding about a topic that could help you to achieve your own dreams?

- Learning is a lifetime occupation. Choose a path of continual improvement; immerse yourself in knowledge. And recognise that knowledge also comes from within. Ask yourself: what did I learn about myself today?

◀◀◀ LEVERAGE YOURSELF

CHAPTER 8
Find your niche.

CHAPTER 8 ▶▶▶

In his book *Crazy Times Call for Crazy Organizations*, Tom Peters asks us to imagine the first focus group that gathered to review the prototype for Post-it Notes.

> "Folks," the suave marketer began, "what I have here are little squares of yellow paper. They have glue on one side. Not very good glue. I mean, it doesn't stick very well. It sort of sticks, but, you know, then it doesn't. Well, this thing is going to replace paper clips. We think it will be a $1 billion market someday."
>
> Would you have bought that act? Don't be silly. Can you live without Post-its today? Maybe, but would you want to? [84]

It's easy to forget that the humble Post-it Note is a recent innovation. Those little sticky squares of paper seem more closely related to workplace antiquities like the stapler and the hole-punch than integrated chips and circuits.

In actual fact the Post-it Note was only launched in 1980, ten years after its genesis in 1970, when 3M scientist, Spencer Silver, developed a new adhesive which stuck to objects, but could easily be lifted off. It was super weak instead of super strong.

> "Mining for niche markets can turn up gold."

No one knew what to do with the stuff, until four years later when Silver's 3M colleague, Arthur Fry, was singing in his church choir. Before each service, he placed tiny slips of paper into his hymn book to mark the songs the choir would sing that day. But Fry had trouble keeping the bookmarks in place; every time he stood up to sing, the slips fluttered from his hymnal. All at once,

Fry remembered Silver's adhesive. If he applied some of Silver's adhesive to his tiny slips of paper, his problem would be solved. Success! With the weak adhesive, the markers stayed in place, yet lifted off without damaging the pages.

A brilliant idea, and yet so simple. In his article celebrating twenty-five years of Post-it Notes, Greg Beato wrote that "Post-it Notes were pretty much the greatest invention since cigarettes. People used them at work, they used them at home, they used them everywhere — and they didn't give you cancer." [85]

> **"Whether you're selling your product at your local market or on the Internet, the principle is still the same: find your niche."**

This story illustrates a truism in today's business world: mining for niche markets can turn up gold.

Whether you're selling your product at your local arts and crafts market or in the global marketplace of the Internet, the principle is still the same: find your niche. Many of today's most successful companies have stopped marketing to the broad customer categories of the past and instead reach out to narrowly-focused groups, using a strategy called 'niche marketing'.

Niche marketing gained currency through Donald K Clifford, Jr. and Richard E Cavanaugh's 1986 work, *The Winning Performance*, which studied 6,117 small companies that had grown four times faster than the Fortune 250.[86] Ninety per cent of these firms, the authors found, competed in small market niches. All were customer- rather than sales-driven. All developed new products with the end-user in mind, and all concentrated on advertising to — and generating repeat sales from — not just any customer, but a small, credit-worthy, qualified group.

CHAPTER 8 ▸▸▸

Clifford and Cavanaugh suggested a series of steps that any company — one-person garage operations or global conglomerates — can take to adopt niche marketing for themselves:

- Compile a comprehensive list of your prospects and customers.
- Narrow the list to a profitable group you believe you can serve better than the competition.
- Create a profile of the traits common to these customers, such as sales volume or location.
- Use this profile to tailor products, services and advertising to your niche market and qualify new prospects.
- Be prepared to experiment with several niches before finding the one that fits your company best.

> "Picking the right segment of the market is vital."

Picking the right segment of the market is vital to not just your success, but your business survival. While niche marketing is often considered the domain of small, agile companies who can react to customer demands more quickly than the global giants, even the big end of town is embracing niche marketing, by refining and targeting their product offerings to different buyer groups.

Nike, for instance, cornered the athletic footwear market by identifying a dozen niche markets within their market — such as basketball, running, tennis and water sports — and designing and marketing products for each of those sports. Nike went further, by segmenting those segments and offering specialised models within those sports (think Air Jordan basketball shoes).

New business owners can learn from Nike's success story. Most new players try to market to everyone in the expectation that they'll gain lots of business. This theory is like throwing mud against a wall and hoping some of it will stick.

Instead, savvy business people are harnessing the power of niche marketing. After years training and competing in arcane martial arts such as the Chinese grappling art of Shuai-Chiao, American Matt Furey wrote a book called *Combat Conditioning* specifically for people preparing for martial arts competitions.[87]

> "Don't throw mud against a wall and hope some of it will stick."

Had he focused on promoting his book in his hometown, or doing the speaking circuit from state-to-state, he may have sold a couple of thousand books. I mean, how big could the market for such a book be? But with the global reach of the Internet, Furey has been able to tap into an international market of people wanting to get in shape. He's selling several million dollars worth of e-books every year. Who would have thought it possible in the era before the information superhighway?

Be relevant

In the 1989 movie, Field of Dreams, Ray Kinsella (played by Kevin Costner) hears a voice: "If you build it, he will come." With the voice comes a vision of a baseball diamond in the middle of his Iowa cornfield. Ray listens to the voice and builds the baseball diamond, only to face failure and potential bankruptcy. It seems all is lost, when James Earl Jones rallies him with his famous soliloquy:

CHAPTER 8 ▸▸▸

"People will come, Ray. They'll come to Iowa for reasons they can't even fathom. They'll turn up in your driveway, not knowing for sure why they are doing it. They'll arrive at your door as innocent as children longing for the past. 'Of course, we won't mind if you look around,' you'll say. 'It's only 20 dollars per person.' They'll pass over the money without even thinking about it — where it is money they have and peace they lack. And they'll walk out to the bleachers in shirtsleeves on a perfect afternoon and find they have reserved seats somewhere along one of the baselines where they sat when they were children and cheered their heroes and they'll watch the game. And it will be as if they dipped themselves in magic waters. The memories will be so thick, they'll have to brush them from their faces. Oh, people will come, Ray. People will most definitely come."[88]

As the closing credits roll, we see the headlights of a long line of cars heading towards the cornfield. People are coming. Ray's dream has come true.

> "Having a dream does not mean your business will be successful."

I don't need to remind you that real life is not like Hollywood. Having a dream does not mean your business will be successful. People won't purchase your product, they won't buy your book, they won't dine in your restaurant simply because you have a dream.

Browse the business section of any good bookstore and you'll find dozens of volumes that tell you to "find your passion", "follow your heart", "do what you love" and you'll be successful. While this philosophy has its merit, there's something more important than simply finding your passion and following it. First, you must find something that people want. You must be relevant.

And while you'll find dozens of books with insights about integrated marketing, tips on how to write SWOT analyses, determine your unique selling point (USP) or segment your database, ultimately it comes down to knowing your customer. What is your typical customer profile? And how are you going to reach them?

It's boring but true: you need to do your homework. If you're starting a nappy cleaning service, make sure you're living in Nappy Valley, not God's Waiting Room. Relevance means asking yourself: "who needs my services?"

When opportunity knocks, you don't have to grab it. My Uncle Jack used to say that "the bargain of the century comes by once a week, so you don't have to worry about catching the first one." There's opportunity all around us and until you realise that you're surrounded by opportunity, you'll grab the first one that appears. However, if you understand you're surrounded by opportunity all the time and that, in fact, the ever-changing world just provides more and more of those opportunities, then you might step back a little bit and take the time to find the one that fits your parameters.

> "When opportunity knocks, you don't have to grab it."

A few years ago, Mary and I identified a suburb in our city that didn't have a bakery, so we decided we'd open up one. While it didn't really fit the criteria of what might be a reasonable success for us (we weren't bakers, for instance), we decided there was a need. We should have said to ourselves: "okay, that's just one opportunity out of a thousand we're going to see this year," and kept looking for the one that was spectacular. Instead, there was a hole in the market and we tried to fill it. Our only problem was

CHAPTER 8 ▸▸▸

someone else had the same idea and two weeks after our bakery opened, a competitor set up shop up the street (and we knew nothing about it until they put their sign up). Now there were two bakeries in a suburb that had operated just fine without one.

The annals of history are littered with stories of businesses that went bust because the owners didn't do their homework. Establish if there is a market for your product or service first, not after you've designed your logo, launched your website and watched your bank balance remain in the red for six months. Don't rely on the fact that you think it's a good idea. Investigate your competitors, find out what makes them stand out from the crowd, ask people what they want, survey your potential customers, analyse your market.

I'm always amazed that our education system encourages young people to consider careers in industries with the most job prospects, yet doesn't teach them to apply the same skills to assessing business opportunities. Career advisers, teachers and parents will all say that it's important to look for careers with growth potential, good salaries and job advancement. Whether it's dentistry or dancing, cartography or Chinese medicine, the smart thing to do is see whether there'll be jobs out there when you finish your degree or diploma. You need to apply this same thinking to your business ideas.

> **"Your USP is the heart of your business, so you need to be able to state it."**

What is going to make your business stand out? You need to answer your customers' question: "Why should I do business with you instead of your competitors?" Your USP is the heart of your business, so you need to be able to state it. If you can't, then your customers won't understand it either.

The battle of the car hire companies is a great example. Avis needed a marketing approach, and a USP, that would give it a market advantage against Hertz, who was well ahead in terms of size and market share. Their USP captured attention: "We're number two. We try harder." Their product was the same as Hertz's but they positioned themselves as the company that would work harder and give better service and better rates. When customers reached for their wallets, the implication that Avis would try harder — would make life easier for them — was appealing. And Avis reaped the rewards.[89]

Once you've identified your USP you can use that repetitively in your sales, marketing, advertising and promotions to build your customers' identification of your company with your product or service. Not only will your USP clearly differentiate your business in the eyes of your current and potential customers, it will focus you and your team on delivering the promise of the USP, helping to improve your internal performance.

> "A market is never saturated with a good product, but it is very quickly saturated with a bad one."

While research should be your first step, most people ignore this — not because research is hard, but because they don't want to face the fact that their idea — their dream — might not work. The trouble is, in not doing your homework, you're only delaying the inevitable.

If your business idea isn't going to work, it isn't going to work. Homework will simply save you a lot of time, money and pain. And Henry Ford once wisely remarked: "a market is never saturated with a good product, but it is very quickly saturated with a bad one."

CHAPTER 8 ▸▸▸

I'll tell you who the loneliest person in the world is: the solitary bloke in the shop that sells vinyl records. There he is. He's busy buying and selling something that's no longer relevant. Sure, he has a passion for vinyl records. Sure, he knows everything there is to know about his product. But here's a man who is in business because he's passionate about his hobby, not because it is a viable, vibrant business opportunity. So, there the records sit, along with him, in the shop. Thousands of vinyl records that no one, except a miniscule group of vinylophiles, wants to buy anymore.

> "Find the market first, then write the book, create the product or open the shop."

Don't be like the glassblower who writes a book about glassblowing and only then thinks about how she's going to market it. All you'll be left with is hot air. Find the market first, and then write the book. I have an associate who invests a lot of time investigating just what information people are searching for on the Internet before he writes a word. He doesn't put pen to paper (or fingers to the keyboard) until he knows exactly what people want to know.

Another client of mine has made a career out of eBay. She monitors the most popular items on eBay, what's selling well, what isn't, and then hunts down popular items to sell in her online shop. She resists the impulse to buy something, simply because she likes the look of it. Instead, she does her homework: is this something my customers will want? Is there a market for this?

Had I done my homework and researched what my potential customers were looking for in the '90s, my business would have made millions. It's easy to see what people want in hindsight. But it's a bit late to capitalise on what customers wanted back in 1994. Instead, I have to know what they want now.

We didn't know what our customers wanted because we never did our homework. Our attitude was that we'd find out what they wanted after we found the customers. As a result, we only got to ask the people who had already made a decision to seek out personal development.

So, spend the time identifying and estimating the size of your target market. Determine whether or not the customer base is large enough to support your business or new product idea. Remember, it's simply not enough that people like your business concept. There must be enough target buyers on a frequent-enough basis to sustain your company sales, spending and profits from year to year. While the idea of an indestructible toothbrush may seem like a winner, you'll need to consider that people may only need to purchase it once in a lifetime. Are there enough people out there wanting to purchase one everlasting toothbrush to sustain your business? Or are you better off looking for something that everyone needs eventually, like funeral services?

> "It's simply not enough that people like your business concept."

CHAPTER 8 ▸▸▸

> ### A new business in sixty minutes
>
> Starting up a business needn't be that difficult. You can start right now, and it will only take you about an hour. Here's how:
> - Go to your computer and open Google. Key in "hot business idea" and copy the ones that intrigue you.
> - Then go to www.trendwatching.com and see what's hot right now. Copy down any of those that spark your interest too.
> - Take your top three ideas and see whether they have a market. The best way to do this is check the number of pages that include the term that interests you. Suss out your competitors too.
> - Now, jot down a simple business plan — what would you need to do to get this idea off the ground?
> - Now act on it.
>
> There you have it. Simple as that.

Innovate!

In a world where change is the only constant, innovation is the new black. It's always in fashion, you can wear it anywhere and it goes with everything. It's also the most powerful engine for business growth and success.

The authors of the BT Technology Timeline say that the next fifty years of change will happen in five to ten years. Could you predict what you'd be doing today five years ago? And what you will be doing in five years time? [90]

Don't fall into the trap of believing that everything clever, useful or profitable has already been invented. Jay Abraham, in *Getting Everything You Can Out of All You've Got*, reminds us that the human brain, while capable of understanding incredibly complex and intricate concepts, is also sometimes unable to recognise the obvious and simple.

"Ice cream was invented in 2000 BC. Yet it was thirty-nine hundred years later before someone figured out the ice-cream cone," he says.

"Meat was on the planet before humans. Bread was baked in 2600 BC. Nevertheless, it took another forty-three hundred years for somebody to put them together and create the sandwich.

> "The human brain is sometimes unable to recognise the obvious and simple."

"And the modern flush toilet was invented in 1777, but it wasn't until 1857 that somebody thought up toilet paper." [91]

It's hard to believe someone didn't think of these products sooner — the connections seem so obvious. Abraham calls these previously hidden opportunities 'breakthroughs'.[92] Malcolm Gladwell calls these 'tipping points' — "the levels at which the momentum for change becomes unstoppable."[93] A tipping point is the moment of critical mass, the boiling point at which "ideas and products and messages and behaviours spread like viruses".[94]

Every now and then, a technological innovation or idea comes along that is so profound and powerful it changes the world. The printing press, the light bulb, the automobile, the personal computer. It doesn't happen often, but when it does, the world is changed forever.

CHAPTER 8 ▸▸▸

That doesn't mean that your breakthrough needs to be as revolutionary as manned flight or the mobile phone. Many of the most extraordinary ideas come from ordinary people. The father of the World Wide Web, Tim Berners-Lee, for instance, thinks the idea of a 'eureka moment' is a myth.

> I think our creativity is subconscious. It happens slowly... it's not that you are really clever and you just thought it up, it's because you've been washing dishes, skiing, talking to people, reading up, concentrating on different aspects of the problem. My hunch is that Archimedes spent a week thinking about the displacement of water, then eventually it came to him. I don't believe it came to him in his bath. It's a nice story.[95]

> "Many of the most extraordinary ideas come from ordinary people."

Sometimes, a slight adjustment to a product or service can be all it takes to make your million. In *Cracking the Millionaire Code*, for instance, Mark Hansen and Robert Allen share the story of the 2004 Olympics in Athens, when the world's top eight swimmers faced each other in the Men's butterfly final.

In this race, the gold medal winner, Michael Phelps, broke the Olympic record by swimming four one-hundredths of a second faster than the silver medal winner. In a snap, he had gold. In fact, all eight hands touched the wall within 1.31 seconds of each other — meaning that any of the eight could have been the victor in the blink of an eye.

"Now, think about how a few tiny adjustments could propel your business from last place to first place," Hansen and Allen say. "One well-worded ad, one well-researched product improvement, one well-respected endorsement, one well-heeled partnership. Just one. Think of it. One. Uno. Un. Eins. Ichi. One tiny little tweak." [96]

Apple gave their product — the iPod — one little tweak and presented the world the iPod Shuffle. For those who've been living under a rock for the last ten years, the iPod Shuffle 'lets you wear 500 songs on your sleeve'. You simply clip the MP3 player onto your jeans and plug in the headphones. With no screen and minimal control, songs are played randomly.

So, how do you turn a product that provides the consumer with little choice into something super cool? The iPod Shuffle's marketing slogans across the Apple site make it clear: "Enjoy uncertainty" ... "Life is random" ... "Choose to lose control". And sure enough, soon every Gen Y is talking about the white-knuckle ride of random listening and Apple has their best selling product in the iPod suite.

> "What's between your ears is more important than the capital you bring to a project."

What's between your ears is more important than the capital you bring to a project. When renowned body language expert Allan Pease published *Everything Men Know About Women*, it became an instant best seller. Touted as a book based on years of research and interviews with thousands of men, and the most complete picture ever revealed of men's knowledge of women, it was also the easiest book for Pease to write. In fact, it took him no time at all.

How did he do it? He didn't write a line. The book is completely blank. 128 pages and not a word on them. Pease found an idea and a niche market, put the two together, and made a mint. In the words of Larry Page,

CHAPTER 8 ▶▶▶

co-founder of Google, "You don't need to have a 100-person company to develop that idea."

Peter Drucker, the father of modern management, identified seven changes that can be converted into opportunities:

1. An unexpected success or failure in your own enterprise, in a competing enterprise, or in the industry.
2. A gap between what is and what could be in a market, process, product or service.
3. Innovation in a process, product or service, whether inside or outside the enterprise or its industry.
4. Changes in the industry structure and market structure.
5. Demographics.
6. Changes in mind-set, values, perception, mood or meaning.
7. New knowledge or a new technology.[97]

> **"You don't need to have a 100-person company to develop that idea."**

Here's an example: by inventing the assembly line production method for making cars, Henry Ford demonstrated that he was a great innovator (opportunity #3). However, Ford's inflexibility ("You can have any colour, as long as it's black") created the opportunity for General Motors to eventually overtake Ford by producing more models in different shapes and colours (opportunity #6). General Motors recognised a shift in the mindset of automobile customers, and created products that responded to those customers' changing needs. So, how could one of these seven changes be a chance for you to innovate?

Solve people's problems

Your business needs to be about more than just making money. A successful business starts with the desire to provide a solution to other people's problems. Why? Because, not only do you enrich the world by enriching the lives of your customers, but because products or services that solve problems will always be popular. Most people could take or leave disease prevention products, but we'll all pay whatever it costs to get the chiropractor to fix a bung back.

The most significant invention since the printing press was developed by a man trying to solve a problem. "Partly I invented the Web for myself because it was something I needed," says Tim Berners-Lee. "A lot of ideas, such as the spreadsheet, were developed by geeks who needed them. I needed this. I wanted it for my job." [98]

> **"Our business is a very obvious example of helping to solve people's problems - both literally and figuratively."**

Our society is, as a rule, cash rich and time poor. We live in the information age — the problem being that most people have an oversupply of it. Mary's and my business, like many others, simply takes latest, leading-edge material and packages it into easy-to-use, simple-to-apply parcels that make our customers' lives easier to live.

Could someone in one of our workshops source the information, evaluate it, experiment with results and then apply it themselves? Absolutely! But is it more effective to buy that knowledge in quick, effective bits? You bet!

Our business is a very obvious example of helping to solve people's problems — both literally and figuratively. But every successful business, whether it's a dentistry practice or a travel agency, is doing that too.

CHAPTER 8 ▸▸▸

In 1954, American psychologist Abraham Maslow explored what energises, motivates and sustains human behaviour. He hypothesised that the needs of all human beings fit into five broad categories: the physiological needs, the needs for safety and security, the needs for love and belonging, the needs for esteem and the need to actualise the self.[99]

Maslow took this idea further and created his now famous hierarchy of needs. According to Maslow, some needs take precedence over others. He argued that as people's needs change, they move up their 'hierarchy of needs'. For example, if you are hungry and thirsty, you will seek out water before food — a person can survive for weeks without food, but only a few days without water. Therefore, thirst is a stronger need than hunger.

Once basic needs like food and shelter are taken care of, then the individual seeks higher level needs (such as money to maintain survival, belonging to a group). Conversely, if lower level needs again become unsatisfied, then people will tend to focus on that. In other words, people are unlikely to be concerned about their personal reputation when they are trying to escape from a burning building — the first priority is more likely to be personal survival!

> "Each time you sell your product, you sell something tangible as well as an abstract concept of that product."

Maslow's theory holds true when looked at in the light of your customers' needs. Each time you sell your product, whatever it may be, not only are you selling something tangible, but also an abstract concept of that product. You're selling an emotion, or filling an emotional need. A man holding the keys of his new BMW is not buying a car. Why would he buy a BMW when he can get away much cheaper with a Toyota, which is more efficient to run and easier to fix? Instead, he's making a statement about himself, and how he feels by purchasing the prestige that goes along with owning a status vehicle. Similarly, a woman spraying herself with Chanel No 5 may say she loves the scent, but really she loves the way it makes her feel.

> "People are looking specifically at niches that solve their problems."

The more levels of the hierarchy a product seems to satisfy, the more consumer demand for that product. The more you can appeal to the lower levels of unfulfilled needs in a person's life, the more successful you will be. But, again, this means knowing your customer. If your product promises to fulfil a self-esteem need, it's useless to promote it to people living in the ghettoes of Soweto, where personal safety is more of a priority than personal fulfilment.

As more people go online looking for answers (from "where do I put the apostrophe?" to "who is the nearest mechanic in my neighbourhood" to "how do I overcome depression" and everything in between) these people are looking specifically at niches that solve their problems. Our business can help some people, but there's a myriad of other competitive, complementary and completely different organisations out there that are also tapping into the seemingly endless supply of prospects.

Goodbye Pareto Principle

A common rule of thumb, which has be applied to everything from the clothes you wear to how you manage your time, is that 80 per cent of a reward comes from 20 per cent of the effort.

CHAPTER 8 ▶▶▶

The observation was first made by Italian economist Vilfredo Pareto, who noticed that 80 per cent of Italy's wealth was owned by 20 per cent of the population. In conducting surveys in a variety of other countries, he discovered that a similar distribution applied.

Since then, the 80:20 rule has been applied to stock control, logistics management, computer science and, of interest to us, sales and marketing. In his 2007 bestseller, *The 4-Hour Workweek*, Tim Ferriss recommended firing the 80 per cent of your customers who take up the majority of your time and focusing on the 20 per cent who make up the majority of your profits.[100]

His idea is based on the premise that by identifying that key 20 per cent of your market that would make you the most profits, you could sell much more product with much less effort.

> "Niche products on the Internet don't seem to stick with the Pareto Principle."

But while Ferriss' fans are losing the lion's share of their customers, researchers at the Sloan School of Management at the Massachusetts Institute of Technology have found that niche products on the Internet don't seem to stick with the Pareto Principle. Almost 40 percent of revenue at Amazon.com is made up of obscure book titles not even carried on retail shelves, for instance.[101]

With that in mind, Chris Anderson, editor of *Wired* magazine, developed his Long Tail theory, arguing that the vast percentage of products that usually get short shrift in the 80-20 world could, on the Internet, outdo the sales volume of all the mainstream market leaders.[102]

Since Anderson's book was published in 2006, researchers at Sloan have examined several years of sales data at a private-label women's clothing company that sold the same merchandise both online and through mail order catalogues. Researchers found that while catalogue sales stood by the Pareto Principle, customers purchased a significantly wider variety of clothing online. After discovering this, executives overhauled their marketing tactics, sending fewer printed catalogues to top online customers.

With all this technical talk of 80:20 rules, hierarchies of need and long tails, you could be forgiven for feeling confused about what it all means. Don't. It all boils down to a simple concept. Peter Drucker once said that a leader should first ask the question "how can I best serve?" Keep that in mind when you're identifying your niche. Pretend you are one of your customers and ask "how can I best serve you?"

> **"Pretend you are one of your customers and ask "how can I best serve you?"**

CHAPTER 8 ▸▸▸

> **Case study:**
> **What do you want out of life?**
>
> "What do I want out of life?" This was the question that rattled around in Mick Cornish's head for many years, as he moved from one successful career to another.
>
> From humble beginnings — he was the only one of five kids to complete Year 10 — Mick started his working life as an electrician, first in Orange and then in Sydney. He rapidly built skills and experience, and before he was 21 was teaching first year apprentices.
>
> While the itinerant life had its freedoms, Mick soon decided to settle down, choosing to study to become a chiropractor at one of the world's best universities in Atlanta, Georgia. But, always the country boy at heart, home beckoned and Mick returned to Australia with Noelle to establish a chiropractic practice in Orange.
>
> Life was great. "I was married to the girl I loved, I had a beautiful son, Jack, and a booming business that only required a personal commitment of 24 hours a week. We wanted for nothing as a family — there was always plenty of money and plenty of time together."
>
> All this changed in November 2004, when a life-altering event made Mick question his "place on this earth, and what I'm here to do."

All this changed in November 2004, when a life-altering event made Mick question his "place on this earth, and what I'm here to do."

Mick was the pilot of a plane that crashed on a windy descent to the runway. Noelle, five-year-old Jack and his 80-year-old mother were all on board. The plane was split in two, but miraculously, all four of them walked away.

The crash shook Mick up. In fact, it made him rethink his entire life. "I began to ask myself: 'If I died tomorrow, am I living my true potential today? I didn't know the answer to that. Something that kept resonating in my head was the voice of Paul Blackburn, who I'd met a few months previously at a short workshop."

Mick embarked on a personal development journey with me, and, as he says "learned to ask great questions of myself." In asking the great questions, great answers were revealed.

Mick realised that while he was very happy in his lifestyle, he wasn't fulfilled.

"While my life as a chiropractor gave me some level of career satisfaction, there were days when I wasn't excited. I knew I could expect nothing new, challenging or exciting. And I wanted to wake up each day with my first thought: what opportunities are out there for me today?"

CHAPTER 8 ▸▸▸

> "Then one morning, we were sitting on our back deck having breakfast when Noelle asked me: 'If we sold the business, what would you do?' I didn't know, but I immediately felt excited. I knew if I sold my business I would give myself the opportunities and the possibility of finding personal fulfilment."
>
> What was the worst thing that could happen? "A bank manager could take away our belongings, but couldn't take us away from each other," Mick says. "We understood that, and so it gave us permission to have a go."
>
> Mick sold his chiropractic business and became a Master Coach with us in 2007. He now trains other people to become success coaches, and helps people to realise their full potential. Quite simply, he's found his niche.[103]

Things to think about…

- Having a dream does not mean your business will be successful. You must also be relevant. Be honest with yourself. Who needs your product or service? Who would respond to your idea?

- Do your homework. Is there a market for your idea? What is going to make your business stand out from the crowd?

- If your business idea isn't going to work, it isn't going to work. Homework will simply save you a lot of time, money and pain. A market is never saturated with a good product, but it is very quickly saturated with a bad one.

- The bargain of the century comes by once a week. Don't try to grab the first opportunity that comes your way.

- Be innovative. You don't need to have a Eureka moment. Instead, think about how you could improve on an existing product or service.

- A successful business starts with the desire to provide a solution to other people's problems. Ask yourself: how can I best serve?

CHAPTER 9
Stretch your prices.

CHAPTER 9 ▶▶▶

While the concept of elasticity has an extraordinarily wide range of applications and can keep economics boffins busy for years, an understanding of elasticity is useful to understand the dynamic response of supply and demand in a market.

If your business is considering a price hike, for instance, you need to examine whether demand for your product is highly elastic. If it is, you may see sales fall sharply, and profits with it. On the other hand, you may find that a price cut does not increase sales if demand for your product is price inelastic.

Let's break this down. Economists say that, for most standard goods and services, a drop in price equals an increase in quantity. So, when sunglasses are on special, we'll buy two for the price of one.

Of course, when the price of sunglasses goes up, we're less inclined to purchase a pair each season. So, the demand for the product is highly elastic, moving in response to changes in price.

> "If your business is considering a price hike you need to examine whether demand for your product is highly elastic."

In contrast, goods and services for which no substitutes exist are generally inelastic. Take demand for antibiotics, for example. If you need a super drug to kill a potentially lethal infection, you'll be willing to pay whatever is necessary rather than die. Whether it's $200 or $2,000, you're going to find the money. In this case, demand for the product is highly inelastic – that is, it is unaffected by movements in price.

Another major factor affecting price elasticity is the budget share of an item. Something that costs $3 (such as a chocolate bar) can have its price raised by 20 per cent without provoking a blink, but the same increase for a $30,000 item (say, a car) would be agonised over. The same increase for a $300,000 item (a house — if you're lucky!) can have a significant impact.

What about rubber bands, which are, of course, elastic? Can they also be inelastic? According to economists, yes, because no one buys more of them when their price goes down, or fewer when their price rises. When was the last time there was a run on rubber bands? So, to an economist, rubber bands are inelastic elastics.

All of this comes down to one thing: find a product or service that people want so much that the cost doesn't matter to them.

Let's look at the airline industry as a good example. When an airline is determining its fares, it divides up the number of seats, which determines much it costs for each person to get on the plane. The airline number crunchers look at their profit margins, and then work out how many people they need on the plane to break even.

> "Find a product or service that people want so much that the cost doesn't matter."

But when you get down to the last seat on the plane, is that seat worth more?

The person who wants that seat will compare the cost of the seat to the result it achieves. So, if a Launceston lawyer needs to be at a court case in Melbourne, and it's going to cost him twenty thousand dollars if he loses the court case, then $1,000 for a seat probably sounds reasonable.

With this in mind, we need to move away from the model that says that

CHAPTER 9 ▸▸▸

the seat is worth a set amount. What people buy is the result. The person wanting that last ticket is saying, "I need to be in Melbourne. Don't bother me with the details; just get me to Melbourne."

> **"Price positioning comes down to confidence."**

The concept we are exploring here is perceived value. I once coached a massage therapist who was charging $50 an hour for his massage services. When I suggested he needed to raise his price to $100, he said he felt like he'd be ripping people off. "But would they feel ripped off if you gave them a $100 massage for $80?"

When somebody consults a massage therapist with a health complaint, they don't consider whether $50 is the going rate. They simply want the pain in their back fixed. How much is the pain relief worth? If you've ever been in that situation, you'll know it's considerably more than $50.

Imagine the success of a massage therapist who says, "My massages cost $100, but I guarantee the pain in your back will disappear". Same service. But is someone going to pay the extra $50 if they get a guarantee that the pain will go away? You bet.

Price positioning comes down to confidence. If you believe in yourself and your product, then you'll feel confident asking for what it's worth.

Here's another example. When I'm taking on new coaching clients, I tell them "if you sign up to see me once a month for a twelve month contract, it's $440 a month. If you want to turn up whenever you feel like it, it's $1,000 an hour." The benefits to my clients are obvious: I am on call in emergencies. Next time there's disaster, death or divorce on the horizon, I can be there, but at a price. My clients understand that I genuinely want to help, but I may be shifting appointments or cancelling flights, which, when talking about airlines, can be a very expensive business, because, when you change your flight at the last minute, guess how much they charge?

Cost reduction can be costly

Do lower prices equal more customers? Not always. In *Manage for Profit, Not for Market Share*, business strategists Hermann Simon, Frank Bilstein and Frank Luby warn against cutting prices out of sheer enthusiasm for the idea that lower prices will revive a customer's wavering devotion and improve the bottom line.

Any first year economics student will tell you that lower prices result in higher volumes, and because lower prices are an easy way to provide extra value to customers, many companies find the temptation to cut prices hard to resist.

"But resist they should," say Simon, Bilstein and Luby. "Proactive price cuts don't make you different, nor do they make you better off. They make you poorer, unless you have the evidence, the data, and the math to prove otherwise." [104]

> "Proactive price cuts don't make you better off. They make you poorer, unless you have the evidence to prove otherwise."

Before you fly the flag of Wal-Mart, Virgin or Dell Computer and point out that Sam Walton, Richard Branson and Michael Dell became billionaires by selling products at bargain prices, consider this:

CHAPTER 9 ▶▶▶

The reason you can neither quickly nor easily replicate the success of [these companies] is that they have achieved a cost advantage so large that no company could easily rival them. They also baked this advantage into their business model from Day One. There can only be one cost leader in the industry. To have Wal-Mart's ability to offer low prices, you would need a significant and sustainable cost advantage. We doubt that you have that advantage now, nor will you achieve it in the short term, if ever. If you operate in a mature industry in which competitors offer similar products based on similar technology and inputs, it may even be impossible for any company to achieve more than a slight cost advantage.[105]

Manage for Profit, Not for Market Share examines what happened when Universal Music Group (UMG), which controlled roughly one-third of the North American market for recorded music, announced in September 2003 that it had slashed the suggested retail prices and wholesale prices of compact discs by up to 30 per cent.

> **"Even with price cuts, it may even be impossible to achieve more than a slight cost advantage."**

UMG said consumer research showed a strong preference for prices well below current levels. It also believed that the threat of online piracy and illegal downloading had fundamentally changed the way many of its customers behaved.

None of its competitors responded with similar price cuts, so UMG's experiment was an opportunity to observe just how strongly a price cut will drive consumer demand. UMG reduced the wholesale prices for most CDs from $12.02 to $9.09, to encourage people to revisit their local music store.

At the time, the Wall Street Journal Europe ran with the headline: "Price Cuts Can't Save the Music Business", arguing that UMG's decision "seems less a savvy attempt to fight back and more a last-ditch effort to avoid losing any further ground." [106]

And it seems they were right.

"Following the price cut, UMG would have needed to ship 33 per cent more CD units just to maintain the same amount of revenue. Achieving the same amount of profit presented an even greater challenge. Depending on what assumptions you make about variable costs, UMG would have needed to sell between 45 and 55 per cent more CDs to break even." [107]

> "Instead of boosting sales and bringing back customers, the price policy had little or no effect at all."

Perhaps most remarkable is that UMG's strategy was aimed squarely at the youth demographic, which had been diluted by free Internet downloads (however illegal) with the click of a button. But Recording Industry Association of America had found that the Generation Y demographic group accounted for only 25 per cent of all music purchases, down from 32 per cent in the early 1990s. In contrast, the age group thirty-five and older accounted for nearly half of all purchases (45.2 per cent), up from roughly a third (33.7 per cent) a decade earlier.[108]

So, UMG's true target demographic was not those iPod-wearing Gen Ys who've never seen a record, much less understand what a broken one would sound like. Instead, UMG's target market was people who pay hundreds of dollars to see U2, the Rolling Stones or the Eagles in concert — people who were hardly going to baulk at paying a few extra dollars for music.

CHAPTER 9 ▸▸▸

A few months after the price cuts, UMG executives "conceded that the price-cut program has not yet been successful."[109] Instead of boosting sales and bringing back customers, the price policy had little or no effect at all. In fact, Universal's market share had actually fallen slightly.

> "Once you have sold a car with high rebates to a customer, he comes back and wants the same deal again."

The "price cuts for everyone" strategy backfired, inflicting permanent damage on UMG's price integrity. Once customers were accustomed to paying the lower price point, they expected it. As Porsche's Chief Executive Officer, Wendelin Wiedeking said, "Once you have sold a car with high rebates to a customer, he comes back and wants the same deal again. You'll never be able to make this customer happy, because he will say your pricing is wrong." [110]

At its simplest level, when the guy at Sandwich Shop A is convinced that people purchase on price alone, he'll start doing specials. Some competitors will react. Let's say, in this hypothetical, the owners of Sandwich Shop B start to skimp on the amount of food they put in the sandwich fillings to save money and bring down the price.

At this point, there's a golden opportunity for a new entrepreneur to enter the market and provide overwhelming value. By filling the sandwiches to bursting point with good quality ingredients, some customers will start to bypass the two cut-price shops in favour of the gourmet sandwich offerings at Shop C.

Case study:
The big squeeze

Why would someone pay $5 for an apple juice when the supermarket stocks them for only a couple of dollars?

When you think you are buying a healthier, fresher alternative, that's when.

An apple juice is an apple juice, but when you can be persuaded that a 750ml low-fat fruity smoothie, bolstered with 'cosmeceutical' supplements such as ginseng, vitamin C and guarana, will do you good, you're more likely to pay top dollar.

Five years ago, your local juice bar was the domain of grocers disposing of wilting product, or mung-bean munching health food operators. All this changed when Janine Allis opened her first Boost Juice Bar in Adelaide in May 2000.

Boost Juice was modelled on the world's biggest smoothie and juice chain, Jamba Juice. The American company opened for business in San Francisco in 1990, cleverly blending the emerging health-food trend with Starbucks-style branding and fast-food chain operating systems.

"The brand is everything," says Allis, who was a publicist for Hollywood studio UPI in a former life. Using clever marketing and psychologically savvy branding (their corporate colours are juicy green, for appetite, and orange for warmth) customers came from far and wide, tempted by the promise of Fun! Tasty! Active! Healthy![111]

CHAPTER 9 ▸▸▸

> Today, Boost is the market leader in the juice and smoothie market in Australia, and with more than 200 franchises and company-owned stories around the world. And Janine Allis? Her apple juice has placed her on BRW's Young Rich List.

Perception is reality

Today's customer doesn't care what's in your product. It's "what's in it for me" that counts.

And more often than not, they're not looking for products and services: they are looking for a result. It may be a greater sense of convenience, safety, confidence, status, pleasure, accomplishment or self-esteem. Whatever it is, it's up to you to determine how your idea solves their problems, and then to communicate to them in a way that makes it clear that your product will make their lives better.

> "It's 'what's in it for me' that counts."

This isn't a new concept: the best advertising campaigns of the twentieth century were selling emotion, rather than products. Nike's "Just Do It" commercials convinced people across the world that simply donning an athletic shoe could change them from couch potatoes to Olympic champions. The image of the rugged, cigarette-smoking Marlboro Man transformed a feminine brand (with a slogan 'Mild as May') into one that became an icon of masculinity in a matter of months. And De Beers' "Diamonds are

Forever" campaign indelibly linked little rocks with betrothal, love and commitment. Even though diamonds can in fact be shattered, chipped, discoloured, or incinerated to ash, would-be-brides across the globe now insist on diamonds.

Everywhere you look there are examples of selling perceived rather than actual benefit. The caravan and camping industry has cleverly focused on the freedom of the highway, rather than the realities of days spent towing a trailer along treacherous tracks through outback Australia. And, as grey nomads across the country line up to buy Winnebagos, they picture themselves cruising up the highway, free from care. In fact, the first thing visitors are asked when they visit the Winnebago website is: "Do you dream of the freedom to travel at a whim to wherever you desire?"

Does it matter that a Winnebago costs half a million dollars and is nothing more than a truck with beds? Does it matter that a quick calculation demonstrates that it's much cheaper to fly to a destination and stay at the Hyatt (in fact, you could spend fifty grand a year for ten years before you'd spend the same amount as on the Winnebago). No way. The person who wants one of these Winnebagos wants the feeling of freedom they associate with it. How much is the dream of endless sunshine and adventures worth? If someone thinks it takes half a million dollars and a truck with beds, then that's what they'll pay.

In his book *Sur/Petition* (beyond competition), Edward de Bono explores the idea of perceived value, and looks at the trials and tribulations of the Swiss watch industry as an example, which, he says:

CHAPTER 9 ▸▸▸

Invented the quartz movement, but did not use the invention because it felt that this invention would kill [its] existing market. Anyone could use the quartz movement, whereas only the Swiss had the skills to make little cogwheels and balance springs. They were right in their thinking… but wrong in their strategy. Watchmakers in Japan and Hong Kong eagerly grabbed the quartz movement, and in one year the sales of Swiss watches dropped by 25 per cent.

What rescued the Swiss watch industry was the very unSwiss concept of the Swatch. The sales of the Swatch at most accounted for only 2 per cent of a $4 billion market, but the Swatch… signalled that telling time was no longer the most important thing in a watch. A $5 watch tells time every bit as well as a $30,000 watch. The Swatch was not selling time so much as fun and costume jewellery.

The Swiss watch industry recovered as soon as it realised it was not selling watches, but jewellery. Indeed, wearing an expensive watch is sometimes the only legitimate way a man can wear, enjoy, and flaunt jewellery. And that has become the nature of the watch business today. [112]

Marketing 101 says that one of the easiest ways to up the perceived value of a product is to up your price. The fashion industry knows this best. Ask anyone dressed in designer labels why they've paid hundreds of dollars for a white T-shirt when they could have purchased a similar one for $10. They'll tell you that their designer glad rags are higher quality, better made and will last longer. If they're honest, they'll say that they are buying the image of the label and the prestige associated with wearing the uniform

> "Marketing 101 says that one of the easiest ways to up the perceived value of a product is to up your price."

of an elite group. The confidence of wearing the Chanel suit or flaunting the Fiorucci sunglasses is of genuine value to those people, affecting their behaviour and even their levels of success.

Napoleon understood this. He was known for presenting his troops with medals instead of money as reward for victories on the battlefield. Sure, it saved the empire money, but Napoleon's gesture cultivated pride and prestige in a way that a few extra dollars, likely wasted on women, beer and cigars, could never achieve.

When is a tissue too good to be used as a tissue? When it's 'Nose Celebrity', a premium Japanese tissue with a price tag not to be sneezed at! Launched in early 2007, Nose Celebrity tissues are far too special for run-of-the-mill noses. At about US$14 a box, blowing your nose on one of these tissues is promised to make you feel like a celebrity.[113]

While this may just be the extreme case of paying through the nose for a premium product (excuse the pun), the value of Nose Celebrity is clear: status, self-esteem or simply being able to stick one in the eye of your competitive friends. If that's what you want from a tissue, then you'll probably feel that $14 is worth the price.

So the question is: how can you upscale, upgrade or upsize your product or service to capitalise on the new consumer?

> **"How can you upscale, upgrade or upsize your product or service to capitalise on the new consumer?"**

In the earth-shaking 1994 book, The *New Marketing Paradigm*, Don Schultz, Stanley Tannenbaum and Robert Lauterborn recorded the seismic shift in the marketplace which has made price almost irrelevant.

CHAPTER 9 ▸▸▸

"Economies of scale no longer guarantee profitability. Giant centralised manufacturing facilities give way to customised, quick-change plants, close to differentiated markets. Niche marketing replaces mass marketing. Suddenly, cost reduction can be costly if it results in reduced customer satisfaction. Quality is no longer determined by manufacturing standards, but rather by customer perception of price/value."[114]

Today, dollars are only one part of the cost. Someone selling hamburgers may not just be competing with another burger vendor selling his products for a few cents more or a few cents less. "It's the cost of time to drive somewhere, the cost of conscience to eat meat at all, the cost of guilt for not treating the kids. Value is no longer the biggest burger at the cheapest price. It's a complex equation with as many different correct solutions as there are sub-sets of customers." [115]

> **"Value is no longer the biggest burger at the cheapest price. It's a complex equation with as many different correct solutions as there are sub-sets of customers."**

There are times when even the most tight-fisted customer will be prepared to pay more for a product or service. For instance, when you're in the market for a bricklayer to help you build your new home, who would you prefer? The brickie who, when asked what he's doing, scoffs "laying bricks, of course"? Or the brickie who turns to you and says, "I'm building a cathedral"?

Both bricklayers and doing the same task — they're laying bricks. But bricklayer number two has a sense of purpose and self-worth. He treats his job as an art form. Which one do you want building your house? And would you be willing to pay a little bit extra to get a better job done? A better house would not just appreciate in value, it would also be better appreciated by the family who lived it.

Price is elastic as long as you increase the value — or the perceived value. I know the number one Lexus dealer in Australia. She sells twice as many Lexus cars as the number two salesperson. What's her secret? She told me, "I'm not very good at selling, so I make sure I give my customers better value."

> "Live by price, die by price."

How does she do that?

"When I take people for test drives I ask them what they like to listen to. If they like The Beatles, when they purchase a car they'll find a Beatles boxed set in the glove box, gift wrapped, with a card that says 'Enjoy your car.' They are so excited that they tell their friends. And those friends drive past other Lexus dealers to come to me."

All this woman does is listen to what her customer wants. Amazingly, people are lining up to buy a Lexus from her because, if you spend $240,000 on a bloody Lexus, apparently a pack of CDs is a big deal.

What's more amazing is that the people who queue for a Lexus don't get to bargain. She's the number one Lexus dealer in the country, and has a long line. If you want to bargain, you can go down the road to the number two dealer.

The moral to the story is simple: don't differentiate yourself on price. Live by price, die by price. Find the target market that appreciates quality over price. The bargain hunters can go find the bargains. Do you want to be

CHAPTER 9 ▸▸▸

in business for the bargain hunters? You can visit the local markets on a Saturday morning and buy a brand new men's business suit for $79. Or you can visit Armani and pay thousands.

The question you must ask yourself is this: is Armani having trouble selling his suits?

Things to think about…

- Find a product or service that people want so much that the cost isn't a factor.

- Price positioning comes down to confidence. If you believe in yourself and your product, then you'll feel confident asking for what it's worth.

- Before you start to play with your prices, think carefully. Is demand for your product or service elastic? If it is, you may see sales fall sharply, and profits with it. Or is it inelastic? In this case, you may find that a price cut does not increase sales.

- Economies of scale no longer guarantee profitability and price cuts don't make you richer. They make you poorer, unless you have the evidence to prove otherwise.

- Price is elastic as long as you increase the value — or the perceived value — of your product or service. Today's customer doesn't care about the details of what's in your product. It's "what's in it for me" that counts.

- Ask yourself: how can I upscale, upgrade or upsize my product or service to capitalise on the new consumer?

CHAPTER 10
Work on the business, not in it.

CHAPTER 10 ▸▸▸

Parkinson's Law states that "work expands so as to fill the time available for its completion." And nowhere is this truer than in business.[116]

Most businesses don't fail to thrive because the owners don't put in the hard yards. They fail because the business owners work too hard — working in the business, rather than on the business.

I'm not the first one to suggest that success comes when you work "on your business, not in it". In *The E-Myth*, Michael Gerber outlines why all business owners should plan for the day when things can run on automatic pilot. Gerber asks business owners to ask themselves:

- How can I get my business to work, but without me?

- How can I get my people to work, but without my constant interference?

- How can I own my business, but still be free of it?

> "Work expands so as to fill the time available for its completion."

- How can I spend my time doing the work I love to do, rather than the work I have to do? [117]

In Chapter 7 on leverage, I explored how many people enter the small business world after an 'entrepreneurial seizure'. A flash of inspiration, a vision of how life could be, or a brilliant idea leads them to quit their jobs and set up shop. But having a dream doesn't equate to business success. Very often, small business people are 'technicians' with a particular technical skill — such as hairdressing, accountancy, IT or dog grooming, you name it — rather than the requisite business skills to make their venture a success.

> "Small business owners fall into the 'DIY trap' - where they must do everything themselves."

So, they do what people normally do: they focus on the day-to-day activities within their comfort zone and ignore the strategic tasks that they find challenging. They "intoxicate themselves with work so they won't see how they really are", as Aldous Huxley puts it.

It's such a massive problem that I have a client whose company teaches hairdressers how to run their businesses instead of working in them. It's a multi-national operation!

As a result, these small business owners fall into the 'DIY trap' — where they must do everything themselves — from handling customer complaints, to balancing the books, to un-jamming the photocopier. And what happens?

They rapidly become ensnared in the urgency, the repetition and the daily grind of the business. They find that they don't own a business, they own a job. It may be a high paying job. It may be a flexible job. It may even be a fun job. But it's still a job. Very soon, the business becomes a trap with no escape route. And it's very difficult to be a dreamer when you can't get out.

I know this from first-hand experience. Mary and I spent the best part of two decades working very hard in our business. We'd roll from one gruelling workshop to the next, thinking that the more seminars we held, the more successful our business would become. And each year, we'd feel like we were making progress, only to discover at the end of the financial year that the results were the same as they'd always been.

CHAPTER 10 ▶▶▶

What finally dawned on us was this: while we were busy in our business, there was no time to look for innovations to take our business to the next level. There was no time to dream and scheme. No time to think expansively about the possibilities. No time to instigate new methods or marketing tactics. And I know that we're not alone. A typical small business has more things to get done in a day than there is time available. In response, we all get out our 'to do' lists and start ticking off the tasks.

> "While you're busy working, you don't see the opportunities, the possibilities."

But while you're busy working, head down, bum up, you don't see the opportunities, the possibilities. You simply don't see the wood for the trees. Even when your business is working well, you are busy trying to make it work better.

Over the years, I've run dozens of time management and leadership workshops. Usually, a group of executives is transported from their offices to our peaceful, bush environment to spend time examining their lives and career directions. With time away from the daily drudgery, people achieve breakthroughs. They find solutions to their business and personal problems without much prompting. Resolutions that have been staring them in the face for years become obvious when they step back.

A similar thing happens when you take a vacation. Logic would tell you, therefore, that it is highly profitable to take holidays. Universities have understood this for years — their academic staff takes sabbaticals, during which time they stop teaching and focus on learning. So, the very concept of stepping out of your life for personal development, or stepping out of your business for business growth is so logical that it simply doesn't make sense that people don't do it. That is, until you look at the average business.

Despite all our best efforts with to do lists, action plans, prioritisation, calendars, state-of-the-art diaries and up-to-the minute timetables, most business people still say there are never enough hours in the day. As the sun sets, they find they have a longer list of things to do than things that got done, so first to go are the activities to sustain, revitalise and re-energise.

In his excellent book, *The Seven Habits of Highly Effective People*, Steven Covey tells us that the reason is simple: because we drive our lives based on urgency, rather than importance.[118]

	Urgent	**Non Urgent**
Important	• Crises • Pressing problems • Deadline-driven projects, meetings, preparations	• Preparation, planning • Prevention • Values clarification • Relationship building • Empowerment
Non Important	• Interruptions, some phone calls • Some mail and reports • Some meetings • Many proximate, pressing matters • Many popular activities	• Trivia, busy work • Junk mail • Some phone calls • Time wasters • 'Escape' activities[119]

Many traditional time management tools focus us on doing the urgent things. However, the more time and energy we spend doing the urgent, the less we have available for the important. And, as you can see from the chart above, many of the important things — those things that will help us to achieve our life's objectives — are not urgent. As a result, they remain at the bottom of the 'to do' list.

CHAPTER 10 ▸▸▸

Interestingly, time management experts suggest we spend up to 60 per cent of our time on tasks that are urgent, but not important. Instead of putting time into the important but non-pressing tasks, we only schedule around 15 per cent of our time for this.

So, where did you spend most time last week?

Decisions about how we spend our time are fairly easy if it is a question of good versus bad. Completing the end of year accounts: good use of time. Surfing the Internet for celebrity gossip: bad use of time. However, the real issue should be good versus best use of time. The struggle ensues when what we do doesn't contribute to what is most important in our lives.

> **"The real issue should not be good versus bad use of time, but good versus best use of time."**

Sometimes we are caused to wake up with a jolt — death, job loss, divorce or poor health. But without reminders such as these most people never really confront the issues; they look for bandaids instead. People become busier and busier and never stop to ask themselves if what they are doing really matters or not. As management guru Peter Drucker put it: "doing the right things is more important than doing things right."

How many people on their deathbed wish they had spent more time at the office? We are constantly making choices about the way we spend our time and then living with the consequences of these choices. However, most of us don't like the consequences because there is a gap between how we are spending our time and what we feel is important in our lives.

What is the solution? We need to look at the underlying beliefs that produce these results. Out of these beliefs come our attitudes and behaviours and, therefore, our results.

Putting first things first

The most effective way to change your beliefs about time may be, as Stephen Covey suggests, to "put first things first". This means making the most important things in your life the most important things in your life.

> "Make the most important things in your life the most important things in your life."

As a primary resource in your business, you need to keep that resource in good condition (particularly if that resource is meant to last a long time). Would you treat a racehorse the way you treat yourself? Would you flog it when it was tired? Would you feed it junk food? Would you prevent it from exercising? No, you wouldn't. Horse owners work hard to get their horses to peak potential, run them in a series of races and then place them in the paddock to 'freshen up'.

But how many business owners invest in themselves? How many business owners find the time to freshen up?

Here's what most business owners do. They work and work, work, work, work, and they're going to take a holiday when they get tired. They just need the time and the money. But rarely do the time and the money coincide. Ask a roomful of business owners when they went on their last vacation. I do frequently, and the answer is usually something like this: a handful will have been on holidays this year, and the rest simply don't go on holidays. How come? Because they're working so hard.

CHAPTER 10 ▸▸▸

What they fail to see is that you can't approach business with the attitude of a marathon runner. Business — and life, for that matter — is a sprint, rather than an endurance event. You run hard, then rest, run hard, then rest. You don't run a long, hard slog uphill without a break. Ever. You may be able to do it for a week, a month, or a year, but eventually something will give — and whether it's your health, your marriage or your sanity, the results aren't pretty. Instead, as Peter Drucker advises "follow effective action with quiet reflection. From the quiet reflection will come even more effective action."

To avoid learning the hard way, find time for activities that will revitalise and refresh both you and your business. While you need rest and relaxation, you also need to extract yourself from the day-to-day operations of your business to sit with your feet up and think about the 'big picture'. You need to be the person who builds, rebuilds, tweaks, tests and thinks about the direction of your company. You need to be the person who prepares your business for growth.

To do this, you need to be organised. Daily planning provides us with a limited view — it focuses us on what is right in front of us and urgency and efficiency take the place of importance and effectiveness.

> **"Follow effective action with quiet reflection. From the quiet reflection will come even more effective action."**

On New Year's Day each year (or before, if you're better organised), you must open your calendar and start to plan your year. Consider the significant events that will occur: anniversaries, birthdays, weddings, births, graduations. Make time for those.

Then ask yourself: when am I going to have my four separate weeks away from the business? You need four of them. When are those things going to occur? This is what Steven Covey calls it "The Big Rocks Principle." To maximise a bucket's capacity, you must put the biggest things in first.

> "The hardest things to fit into your schedule, such as vacations, must be slotted in first."

So, you start by placing the big rocks in the bucket. Then in go the little rocks. Then you pour in the sand, which fills the crevices between the big and small rocks. And finally, when it seems like there's no more room, you pour in some water. So, what would have happened if you had started with the water? The lesson is this: the hardest things to fit into your schedule, such as vacations, must be slotted in first.

For twenty years, a friend of mine would ask me to go skiing with him. Each year, I'd say I was too busy. Each year he'd shrug his shoulders and say "next year". And I'd shake my head and marvel that he had it so easy that he could find the time to go skiing in the third week of August every year. Why the third week of August? Because that's when the ski resorts in Australia offer the most predictably good snow. This friend loved skiing, so he organised his life to be on the slopes each year for the third week of August. While he was able to plan for a refreshing, revitalising week of skiing, I was assuming I'd get around to some leisure time, some time.

Once you've got your big blocks of time marked out, the next thing to do is to look at each month. It's clear that some months are going to be busier than others. As a business owner, you'll know when your peak times are, whether it's the Christmas rush or the end of financial year scramble.

CHAPTER 10 ▶▶▶

Then look at your weekends. The average wage earner has a major advantage over a business owner, because he or she gets four two-day weekends each month. Most business owners don't. If you work on the weekends, you need to find time for yourself during the week. You need time for rest, exercise, a chance to catch up with family, but also time to educate yourself, to think and plan how to improve your business.

> "All intellectual improvement arises in leisure."

Next, look at your week and ask yourself the same question: where is the time for me?

It's important to remember that taking time out of the business doesn't mean that you slack off. This year, Mary and I are on track to achieve our best ever business results, and yet we're having more time out of our business than ever before. It's tempting for people to read this and say, "It's easy for you. You're making heaps of money." I'm suggesting that it's the other way around; we're making more money because we're taking more time off. And, it's in that downtime that we can examine trends, analyse market research, scrutinise our business practice, talk to experts, meet with our mentors, gain feedback from our coaches and customers and think about what we've learned along the way. By taking time out, we have the space to be students in the game of business.

Daydreaming and innovation go hand in hand. Samuel Johnson, who wrote the great English language dictionary of the eighteenth century, once said that "all intellectual improvement arises in leisure." When stumped, Thomas Edison would unfailingly take a nap. US poet laureate Rita Dove once worried that we don't pay enough attention to daydreaming, "without which no bridges would soar, no light bulbs burn, and no Greek warships set out upon Homer's 'wine-dark sea'."[120]

I spent more than twenty years in handcuffs, chained to my business. Now, I can see that, despite the outward air of success, I was leading a frustrating existence because I couldn't find the missing clues that would help me solve the riddle of my business. Having found a few of those missing pieces, I'm now in search of the remaining pieces of the puzzle. And I realise that I won't find them when I'm chained to my desk. I'll find them during the breaks away.

Don't do something — just sit there

Our fast paced, high pressure Western lifestyle has taken its toll. In survey after survey, Americans, Australians and Brits identify stress as their number one health concern today. Nearly 50 per cent of adults in the US, for instance, report high stress on a daily basis.[121] Untreated, stress can seriously affect performance, health and wellbeing.

> "Americans, Australians and Brits identify stress as their number one health concern today."

One of the best stress reduction techniques is meditation. While the ancient art of meditation has been practiced for more than 5,000 years, it is only just beginning to gain acceptance in the medical community for its physical, mental, emotional and spiritual benefits.

For instance, Dr Richard Davidson of the University of Wisconsin at Madison has, among other experiments, used cranial electrodes and MRI scans to study Tibetan monks on loan from the Dalai Lama. His basic finding, published in January 2008, is that the brain functioning of serious meditators is 'profoundly different' from that of non-meditators — in ways that suggest an elevated capacity to concentrate and to manage emotions. He calls meditation a "kind of mental training".[122]

CHAPTER 10 ▸▸▸

Dr Herbert Benson of the Mind-Body Medical Institute, which is affiliated with Harvard and several Boston hospitals, reports that meditation induces a host of biochemical and physical changes in the body, collectively referred to as the 'relaxation response'. This includes changes in metabolism, heart rate, respiration, blood pressure and brain chemistry.

While the stress response releases adrenalin, causing blood pressure, heart rate and breathing rates to increase, the relaxation response has the opposite effect: your heart rate, blood pressure and breathing rates decrease. You feel more relaxed and less anxious, not just during the relaxation process, but also throughout the day.

> "Meditation can help with better performance and productivity."

Companies are cottoning on to the idea that meditation can help with better performance and productivity. A *Fortune Magazine* article from 2007 reported that high-powered executives in America's most successful companies were looking to meditation to help them thrive — or temporarily disconnect from —- today's BlackBerry-obsessed business climate.[123] They've realised that if meditation increases brain-wave activity, improves intuition, sharpens concentration and alleviates aches and pains, then it may enhance their competitive edge.

For instance, Bill George, the former CEO of the world's largest medical technology company, Medtronics, has meditated twice a day for the past 30 years. He says: "Out of anything, it has had the greatest impact on my career." Robert Shapiro, the former head of Monsanto, a multinational food biotechnology company, says that meditation improved his ability to listen and to think creatively.

> "If you are going to be successful, you need the intellectual space to reflect and regenerate."

So, if meditation lays the foundation for better decision-making and communication, is it worth giving it a go? Don't just shrug meditation off as 'boring' and say it doesn't work for you. Find a way to make it work for you. If you are going to be successful, you need the intellectual space to reflect and regenerate.

Sitting in the lotus position doesn't work for me. Instead, I've found that the best way for me to meditate is to be physically active. I rise at 6 o'clock each morning to spend time on my exercise bike. When I have a gig on, I'm on the bike for even longer, because my focus is on mental fitness. I know I need time to myself. I know I need to minimise the mental chatter before a big event, and I know that, without meditation, I won't be calm and centred.

When I stand up in front of a crowd, I have an hour to convince my audience to do something that they have no intentions of doing. It may be facing their fears, stepping out on a limb, daring to do something they've been dreaming about for years. Whatever it is, I need to persuade them that it is possible. In that way, I'm no different from many other business owners that must convince their customer to buy their product or service.

When we examine my persuasive powers, they have nothing to do with the words that I use. Anyone could record my presentation, learn it and then repeat it. So why am I successful? It's not the location, the audience or the other speakers. It's my state of mind.

As a professional speaker, there are an infinite number of variables that can determine or influence a result. The only one that I can influence

CHAPTER 10 ▶▶▶

> "Confidence comes with taking care of the space between your ears."

positively is my state of mind, so that's where I need to place my efforts and energy.

I laugh when I hear my colleagues say "that was a tough crowd". That is just an excuse. Everyone has bad days. But you won't hear Tiger Woods saying he was using the wrong golf clubs on a bad day — he'll talk about his mental preparation.

Look at it another way: I've watched bank shares drop 10 per cent overnight, and wondered "how can banks be worth 10 per cent less today than they were yesterday?" And then, sure enough, a few days later, bank shares are back up again. What's going on? The banks aren't suddenly in more or less trouble. Instead, they are jolted by opinion and emotion. The same is true for me. If I'm going to perform well, then I'm going to need confidence. And confidence comes with taking care of the space between your ears.

Even though there are days when the last thing I want to do is drag my body out of bed and get on that exercise machine, I do it — because I know that meditation translates into money in the bank. Your instinct may be to say "that's a load of rubbish," and sleep in. Fine. Have it your way. If you don't believe that getting up early to exercise and spend time with your own thoughts will make a difference to your results, then don't do it. But for me, being in better condition — mentally and physically — enables me to do a better job. And a better job translates into better financial rewards. When I didn't meditate so regularly — I didn't make so much money.

This is true for people in all walks of life. Whether you are a high flying millionaire or an apprentice, you'll find as your energy and enthusiasm levels increase, so do your ideas and innovations. As you work hard to reach your potential, your colleagues will be inspired by you, your boss will notice you, your company will profit and the promotions and pay rises will follow.

Supermodel Linda Evangelista once said "I don't get out of bed for less than $10,000 a day". But, she didn't reach the top of the elite modelling world by lolling around in bed all day waiting for the talent scouts to knock on her door. She got out there and worked for her dreams. And then, only then, was she able to call the shots.

In life, you must always give before you receive. You can't ask your bank manager to "give me all the interest for the money that I'm going to give you over the next 20 years". You can't ask your boss for your long service leave on your first day at the firm because you're committed to staying the course for 10 years. A plant doesn't grow until you put the seed in the ground. There's no endeavour in life where you get the reward before the effort.

> "There's no endeavour in life where you get the reward before the effort."

The bottom line is to find a meditation method that works for you. Exercise bikes are good for me, so is swimming. Some people like yoga, others prefer Tai Chi; some like to sit in silence, others find that a long run works best. Whatever you choose, the most important thing is to put the time in. Meditation creates more time than it takes, and there's an old saying: "If you can't spend half an hour meditating, you need an hour".

CHAPTER 10 ▸▸▸

Case study:
A magic moment on a train

It's hard to believe that the author of the fastest-selling book of all time had her flash of inspiration while sitting quietly on a train.

But it's true. In 1990, while Joanne Kathleen Rowling was on a four-hour-delayed train trip, the idea for a story of a young boy attending a school of wizardry "came fully formed" into her mind.[124]

"I was going by train from Manchester to London, sitting there, thinking of nothing to do with writing and the idea came out of nowhere and I could see Harry very clearly; this scrawny little boy and it was the most physical rush of excitement. I've never felt that excited about anything to do with writing. I've never had an idea that gave me such a physical response. So I'm rummaging through this bag to try and find a pen or a pencil or anything. I didn't even have an eyeliner on me. So I just had to sit and think. And for four hours, because they train was delayed, I had all these ideas bubbling up through my head." [125]

Rowling says she raced home to her London flat and began writing. But life got in the way, and during the course of writing her first novel, her mother died from multiple sclerosis, she divorced an abusive husband, became a single mother and struggled to raise a child on social security.

> In 1995, Rowling finished her manuscript for Harry Potter and the Philosopher's Stone on an old manual typewriter. The book was submitted to twelve publishing houses, all of which rejected the manuscript. A year later she was finally given a £1,500 advance by editor Barry Cunningham from Bloomsbury, who advised Rowling to get a day job, since she had little chance of making money in children's books.
>
> Since then, the seven Harry Potter books have gained worldwide attention, won multiple awards, and sold nearly 400 million copies. The 2008 Sunday Times Rich List estimated Rowling's fortune at £560 million (US$1.1 billion), ranking her as the 12th richest woman in Britain. Forbes has named Rowling the first author to become a US-dollar billionaire, the second-richest female entertainer and the 1,062nd richest person in the world.[126] And she owes it to a magic moment on a train.

Making the most of time

The dividing line between success and failure is best summed up in five little words: I did not have time. Busyness has become our collective catch-cry, as we try to keep up with a world in hyper-drive, with 24/7 connectivity, information overload and an eye-popping rate of technological change. It's no wonder we often feel it's hard to keep up.

And yet, despite the frenetic pace of change, we are not working longer hours. In fact, we've never had it so good. In Australia, there has been an eight per cent fall in the average weekly hours over the past 30 years, to

CHAPTER 10 ▶▶▶

32.9 hours in 2007. At the same time, real wages have climbed by 37 per cent. So we are, on average, much better off.

The total of working hours in our lives has remained constant — at 130,000 for the past 220 years. But given we live so much longer, this work is now spread out over a longer time frame. A man no longer devotes 24 per cent of the hours in a year to work, as was the standard practice in 1800. In 2008, it will be 12 per cent.

> "We have almost double the leisure time of our ancestors who arrived with the First Fleet."

In the late eighteenth century, most people worked a 60-65 hour week every week of the year — from the age of 13 until death. No long-weekends, no sickies, no paternity leave. These days, taking into account annual leave, public holidays and sick leave, our weekly hours are half that, but we work for twice as many years (50 plus). Formal education means we start working later in life. And most people have the luxury of retirement. So, next time you say there are never enough hours in the day, remember we have almost double the leisure time of our ancestors who arrived with the First Fleet — 43 per cent of our lifetime hours compared with just 23 per cent in 1788.[127]

Mark Twain once observed, "twenty years from now, you will be more disappointed by things that you didn't do than by the things that you did do". If it's true that we all have more time than in any moment in history, then there's really no excuse for not making the most of yours.

Things to think about…

- Most businesses don't fail to thrive because the owners don't put in the hard yards. They fail because the business owners work too hard — working in the business, rather than on the business.

- Ask yourself, how can I get my business to work without me? How can I avoid the DIY trap?

- We all need to put first things first — which means making the most important things in our lives the most important things in our lives. What's most important to you? How are you going to prioritise that?

- What important tasks are you putting off because you are swamped with urgent tasks? What urgent but unimportant tasks could you allocate to someone else?

- Daydreaming and innovation go hand in hand. How will you create the intellectual space you need to reflect and regenerate?

- Taking the time out for meditation can give you a competitive edge.

- The dividing line between success and failure is best summed up in five little words: I did not have time.

CONCLUSION
Look for something bigger than you.

CONCLUSION ▸▸▸

The old Chinese proverb hopes that we'll "live in interesting times". Interesting or not, the early part of the twenty-first century is a comfortable time to live. In fact, it's never been easier to cruise through life.

But in cruising, we're missing out on one of the great experiences in the game of life: challenge. If you look at golf, one of the world's most popular games, you can always play better tomorrow. Regardless of your results today, you can always be better the next time you step out onto the green.

If that is the case, it means that human beings are motivated by challenge. And if we are motivated by challenge, then we owe it to ourselves to seek and embrace life's challenges.

> **"The riskiest thing we can do is not to risk."**

For me, going into business has been one of my life's most daring experiments. The beauty of business is that each and every day I'm up against myself. Whether I'm faring better or worse than yesterday has more to do with what's going on in my head than it does with what's happening on the stock market. And, unlike my friends and family in traditional jobs, I can always fare better tomorrow. Just like golf, every time I walk out onto that course, I can play a little bit better. My results are dependent on me.

With any new adventure there is inherent risks. You may have heard it before, but the riskiest thing we can do is not to risk. Because in not risking, while we make ourselves secure, we lose some of our vibrancy and vitality. The less risk an activity involves, the more chance it has of being ordinary.

◂◂◂ LOOK FOR SOMETHING BIGGER THAN YOU

For 25 years, I've asked crowds from 10 to 10,000 what they would wish for if they were granted just one wish. Consistently, the answer is health, wealth, happiness and positive relationships.

My view?

You don't earn happiness through diligence or good fortune. It's a daily decision made regardless of your circumstances.

Wealth isn't money in the bank. It's the knowledge that you could do it all again.

Health is a gift, appreciated most by those who have battled to achieve it.

And a relationship is the opportunity to meet yourself face to face.

None of us know what our potential is until we must use it. Without risking, without challenging, without daring to stretch myself, I am never going to realise my full potential. Most people discover untapped inner strength only when faced with difficult circumstances. My relationship with my wife, Mary, was set in stone when we spent 18 months living in a caravan together. We had no water and no electricity, but we did have two small children and Mary's elderly mother to look after. We were cramped in a very confined space, with primitive cooking conditions and a not much more than a bucket to bathe in.

In these circumstances, it's fair to say that a relationship is either going to get better or worse. Most people would never risk doing something so challenging. What could possibly be gained from such an experience? If you ask my children — plenty. They'll tell you that many of the golden moments of their lives happened when we lived in a caravan, cooked on an open fire and bathed under the stars.

CONCLUSION ▸▸▸

It's important to have goals and targets. We should never cruise. But equally, we should never let our goals own us. The people in your life are not going to love you more when you make that first million. If you are able to truly realise this, then you are free to dare, to dream, to risk.

So, ask yourself this: what will be my legacy? What will I leave behind on planet earth when I am gone?

For each of us, our motivation for success is going to be different, but whatever your goals and ambitions, it's vital that you find something in your life that is bigger than just you.

> **"Find something in your life that is bigger than just you."**

Those people we most admire in the world — people like Mother Theresa and Nelson Mandela — achieved greatness by focusing on something greater than themselves.

So, what would you do for your loved one that you wouldn't do for yourself?

A wise philosopher once said, "When you help another person get to the top of a mountain, you will arrive there also." I learnt this lesson when I started rising at 4.30am three mornings a week to take my youngest daughter to swimming training. There's no way I'd be crawling out of bed before dawn to exercise myself, but when it came to helping my daughter reach her potential, I jumped out of bed with a spring in my step. And the experience taught me that we each need something outside ourselves, a higher purpose, a noble cause, something to aim for beyond money and status and possessions.

The question is: what is that going to be for you?

◀◀◀ REFERENCES

1. Remarque, Erich Maria, The Black Obelisk, translated by Denver Lindley (New York: Harcourt, Brace-World Inc, 1957) p. 262.
2. Thomas Stanley and William Danko, The Millionaire Next Door, Harper Collins Publishers, Sydney, 1996, p. 232.
3. I Bickerdyke, R Lattimore and A Madge, Business Failure and Change: An Australian Perspective, Productivity Commission Staff Research Paper, AusINfo, Canberra, 2000, p. 20.
4. Mark Hansen and Robert Allen, Cracking the Millionaire Code, Random House, Sydney, 2005, p. 11.
5. Stanley & Danko, p. 1.
6. Stanley & Danko, pp. 3-4.
7. Stanley & Danko, p. 8.
8. Stanley & Danko, p. 13.
9. The World's Billionaires 2008, Forbes.com, viewed 8 July 2008 <http://www.forbes.com/business/billionaires/>
10. Donald Trump and Tony Schwartz, Trump/The Art of the Deal, Random House, New York, 1987, p. 1.
11. World Institute for Development Economics Research of the United Nations University, World Income Inequality Database V2.0c May 2008, viewed 20 June 2008 <http://www.wider.unu.edu/research/Database/en_GB/database/>
12. Stanley & Danko, p. 228.
13. Hansen & Allen, p. 42.
14. Michael E Gerber, The E-Myth Revisited, HarperCollins, New York, 1995, p. 69.
15. Hansen & Allen, p. 5.
16. Jay Abraham, Getting Everything You Can Out of All You've Got, Piatkus Publishers, London, 2000, p. 39.
17. Abraham, p. 39.
18. Arthur C Clarke, The Telephone's First Century - And Beyond: Essays on the Occasion of the 100th anniversary of Telephone Communication, Thomas Y Crowell, New York, 1997, p. 87.
19. Po Bronson, 'What's the Big Idea?', Stanford Magazine online, viewed 8 July 2008 <http://www.stanfordalumni.org/news/magazine/1999/sepoct/articles/bhatia.html>
20. Weinberg [et al.], Perceived goal setting practices of Olympic athletes: an exploratory investigation, The Sport Psychologist, 14(3), 2000, pp. 279-295.
21. Burton [et al.], The goal effectiveness paradox in sport: examining the goal practices of collegiate athletes, The Sport Psychologist, 12(4), 1998, pp. 404-418.
22. Lerner [et al.], The effects of goal setting and imagery training programs on the free-throw performance of female basketball players, The Sport Psychologist, 10, 1995, pp. 382-297.
23. Hansen & Allen, p. 48.
24. Martin Seligman PhD, Learned Optimism: How to Change your Life and Mind, Free Press, New York, 1998, Chapter 10.
25. C Richard Snyder (ed), Handbook of Hope: Theory, Measures, and Applications, Elsevier Science & Technology Books, Chicago, 2000, p. 22.
26. Hansen & Allen, p. 75.
27. Gerber, p. 5.
28. Daniel Goleman, Emotional Intelligence, Bloomsbury Publishing, London, 1996, p. 8.
29. Snarey & Vaillant, How lower- and working-class youth become middleclass adults: The association between ego defense mechanisms and upward social mobility, Child Development, 56(4), 1985, pp. 899-910.
30. Arthur Janov, Primal Healing: Access the Incredible Power of Feelings to Improve Your Health, New Page Books, New Jersey, 2006, p. 216.
31. Tara Bennett-Goleman, Emotional Alchemy: How the Mind Can Heal the Heart, Random House, New York, 2001, p. 81.
32. Joseph E LeDoux, The emotional brain: The mysterious underpinnings of emotional life, Simon & Schuster, New York, 1996, Chapter 1.

REFERENCES ▶▶▶

[33] Friedrich Nietzsche, The Gay Science, Third Book, 1882, Aphorism 270.
[34] For more information on Jason Urbanowicz see: www.createptwealth.com
[35] Nelson Mandela, Long Walk to Freedom. Little, Brown and Company, New York, 1994, Chapter 2.
[36] Henry David Thoreau, Walden, Penguin, Sydney, 1980, p. 10.
[37] Hollywood's Master Storyteller, CNN.com, viewed 7 July 2008 <http://www.cnn.com/CNN/Programs/people/shows/spielberg/profile.html>
[38] Jack Canfield, Mark Victor Hansen & Patty Hansen, Condensed Chicken Soup for the Soul, Health Communications Inc, Florida, 1996, p. 150.
[39] Peter Drucker, Innovation and Entrepreneurship: Practice and Principles, Harper & Row, New York, 1985, p. 43.
[40] Michael Jordan & Tinker Hatfield, Driven from Within, Simon & Schuster, Sydney, 2006, p. 18.
[41] Wikipedia, Donald Trump, viewed 14 July 2008 <http://en.wikipedia.org/wiki/Donald_Trump>
[42] Stephen Covey, The Seven Habits of Highly Effective People, Simon & Schuster, New York, 1989, pp. 219-220.
[43] Stålenheim, Perdomo and Sköns, Military expenditure, SIPRI Yearbook 2008, Oxford University Press, Oxford, 2008, pp. 175-206.
[44] Elisabeth Autore Lacoste and Philippe Chalmin, From Waste to Resource: 2006 World Waste Survey, Rilegatura Paperback, 2007.
[45] Covey, p. 207.
[46] TomPeters! blog, viewed 14 July 2008 <http://www.tompeters.com/entries.php?note=009440.php>
[47] The Body Shop website, viewed 14 July 2008 <http://www.thebodyshop.com/bodyshop/values/support_community_trade.jsp>
[48] Karim Benammar, Abundance and scarcity: concepts and rhetoric in ecology, economics, and eco-ethics, Acta Institutionis Philosophiae et Aestheticae (17), 1999, pp. 91-99.
[49] Katharine Hansen, Foot in the Door: Networking Your Way Into the Hidden Job Market, Ten Speed Press, California, 2000, pp. 16-17.
[50] Stanley Milgram, The small-world problem, Psychology Today (1), 1967, pp. 61-67.
[51] Hansen & Allen, p. 131.
[52] Jure Leskovec and Eric Horvitz, Planetary-Scale Views on an Instant-Messaging Network, Microsoft Research Technical Report, June 2007, p. 2.
[53] Malcolm Gladwell, The Tipping Point: How Little Things Can Make a Big Difference, Little Brown, New York, pp. 34-38.
[54] Gladwell, p. 33.
[55] Gladwell, p. 38.
[56] Memorable quotes from Six Degrees of Separation, Internet Movie Database, viewed 14 July 2008 <http://www.imdb.com/title/tt0108149/quotes>
[57] Bonnie Nardi, Steve Whittaker, and Heinrich Schwarz, It's Not What You Know, It's Who You Know: Work in the Information Age, First Monday peer-reviewed journal on the Internet, (5)5, 2000, viewed 14 July 2008 < http://www.firstmonday.org/Issues/issue5_5/nardi/>
[58] Nardi, Whittaker and Schwarz, 2000.
[59] Rosabeth Moss Kanter. Evolve!: Succeeding in the Digital Culture of Tomorrow, Harvard Business Press, 2001, p. 135.
[60] Leslie Kaplan, Coping With Peer Pressure, The Rosen Publishing Group, New York, 1993.
[61] Jack Welch & Suzy Welch, Winning, HarperCollins Publishers, New York, 2005.
[62] Stanley & Danko, p. 129.
[63] Gerber, p. 10
[64] Gerber, p. 109.
[65] Gerber, p. 85.
[66] McDonald's website, viewed 6 June 2008 <http://www.mcdonalds.com/corp/news/fnpr/2008/fpr_012808.html>
[67] Gerber, p. 85.

◂◂◂ REFERENCES

68. Peter Drucker, The Effective Executive, Harper and Row, New York, 1966, p. 4.
69. Tom Peters, The Tom Peters Seminar: Crazy Times Call for Crazy Organizations, Vintage Books, New York, 1994, p. 161.
70. Peters, The Tom Peters Seminar, p. 10.
71. John Brodkin, IDC report: Data creation outstrips storage for first time, Computerworld, viewed 14 July 2008 <http://www.computerworld.com.au/index.php/id;1049337788>
72. Peters, The Tom Peters Seminar, p. 11.
73. Abraham, p. 348.
74. Wikipedia, Yuichiro Miura, viewed 14 July 2008 <http://en.wikipedia.org/wiki/Yuichiro_Miura>
75. Wikipedia, Eamonn Coghlan, viewed 14 July 2008 <http://en.wikipedia.org/wiki/Eamonn_Coghlan>
76. Jonathan Leake, 60 years on, IQ test tells us how we age, 25 March 2007, Times Online, viewed 14 July 2008 <http://www.timesonline.co.uk/tol/news/uk/science/article1563915.ece>
77. Donald Trump: The Way to the Top, Crown Business, New York, 2004.
78. Donald Wetmore, Time's a Wastin', Training and Development Magazine, ASTD September, 2000, p. 67.
79. Wetmore, p. 67.
80. Wikipedia, Moore's Law, viewed 14 July 2008 <http://en.wikipedia.org/wiki/Moore's_law>
81. Michael Janda, Net starts to overtake TV, 21 May, 2008, ABC Online, viewed 14 July 2008 <http://www.abc.net.au/news/stories/2008/05/21/2251210.htm>
82. Abraham, p. 46.
83. Wikipedia, Rubik's Cube, viewed 9 October 2008 <http://en.wikipedia.org/wiki/Rubik's_Cube>
84. Tom Peters, The Tom Peters Seminar, p. 234.
85. Greg Beato, Twenty-Five Years of Post-it Notes, from The Rake, April 2005, viewed 9 October 2009 <http://www.therake.com/reporting/features/twenty-five-years-post-it-notes>
86. Donald K Clifford, Jr. and Richard E Cavanaugh, The Winning Performance: How America's high-growth midsize companies succeed, London, Bantam Books, 1988, p. 86.
87. Find out more about Matt Furey at www.mattfurey.com
88. Memorable quotes from Field of Dreams, The Internet Movie Database, viewed 9 October 2008 <http://imdb.com/title/tt0097351/quotes>
89. Abraham, pp. 19-20.
90. BT Technology Timeline, viewed 9 October 2008 <www.btplc.com/innovation/news/timeline/index.htm>
91. Abraham, p. 3.
92. Hansen & Allen, p. 235.
93. Gladwell, p. 12.
94. Gladwell, p. 7.
95. Nigel Farnadale, Tim Berners-Lee: a very British boffin, Telegraph.co.uk, 30 March 2008, viewed 9 October 2008 <http://www.telegraph.co.uk/connected/main.jhtml?xml=/connected/2008/03/30/sv_timbernerslee.xml&page=3>
96. Hansen & Allen, p. 203.
97. Hansen & Allen, p. 235.
98. Farndale, 30 March 2008.
99. Abraham Maslow, A Theory of Human Motivation, Psychological Review 50, 1943, pp. 370-96.
100. Timothy Ferriss, The 4-Hour Work Week, Random House, New York, 2007.
101. Eric Brynjolfsson [et.al.], Goodbye Pareto Principle, Hello Long Tail: The Effect of Search Costs on the Concentration of Product Sales, November 2007.
102. Chris Anderson, The Long Tail: Why the Future of Business is Selling Less of More, Hyperion, Chicago, 2008.
103. For more information about Mick Cornish, see: www.mickcornish.com
104. Frank F. Bilstein, Frank Luby, and Hermann Simon, Manage for Profit, Not for Market Share: A Guide to Greater Profits in Highly Contested Markets, HBS Press, 2006, viewed 9 October 2008 <http://hbswk.hbs.edu/archive/6314.html>

REFERENCES ▶▶▶

[105] Bilstein [et al.], 2006.
[106] Brian Carney, Price Cuts Can't Save the Music Business, Wall Street Journal Europe, 22 September, 2003.
[107] Bilstein [et al.], 2006.
[108] 2002 Consumer Profile, Recording Industry Association of America (RIAA), Washington, DC.
[109] Ethan Smith, Music Industry Sounds Upbeat as Losses Slow, Wall Street Journal, January 2, 2004.
[110] Wiedeking's Strategy for Porsche: Image Builds Business, Automotive News, November 18, 2002.
[111] Michelle Griffin, The Big Squeeze, The Age, viewed 10 October 2008 <http://www.theage.com.au/articles/2004/01/31/1075340890745.html>
[112] Edward de Bono, Sur/Petition: Creating Value Monopolies When Everyone Else is Merely Competing, HarperBusiness, New York, 1992, p. 111.
[113] Steve Levenstein, 'Nose Celebrity' Tissues for High Sneezers, InventorSpot, viewed 10 October 2008 <http://inventorspot.com/articles/nose_celebrity_tissues_high_stat_10272>
[114] Don E Schulz, Stanley I Tannenbaum and Robert F Lauterbon, The New Marketing Paradigm, NTC Business Books, Chicago, 1994, pp. 11-12.
[115] Schulz [et al.], pp. 12-13
[116] Wikipedia, Parkinson's Law, viewed 10 October 2008 <http://en.wikipedia.org/wiki/Parkinson's_law>
[117] Gerber, p. 110.
[118] Covey, p. 151.
[119] Covey, p. 151.
[120] Rita Dove, To Make a Prairie, The Key Reporter, Fall 1993.
[121] G Scott Thomas, Where America's most stressful places are, Bizjournal, 11 February 2008, viewed 10 October 2008 <http://www.bizjournals.com/edit_special/62.html>
[122] Richard J Davidson and Antoine Lutz, Buddha's Brain: Neuroplasticity and Meditation, , IEEE Signal Processing Magazine, January 2008, pp. 171-6.
[123] Oliver Ryan, How to succeed in business: Meditate, Fortune, 20 July 2007.
[124] Stephanie Loer, All about Harry Potter from Quidditch to the future of the Sorting Hat. Boston Globe, 18 October 1999.
[125] Harry Potter and Me, BBC Christmas Special, 13 November 2002, transcription viewed 10 October 2008 < http://www.accio-quote.org/articles/2001/1201-bbc-hpandme.htm>
[126] The World's Billionaires 2008, Forbes, viewed 10 October 2008 <http://www.forbes.com/lists/2008/10/billionaires08_Joanne-(JK)-Rowling_CRTT.html>
[127] Phil Ruthven, You never had it so good, Qantas Magazine, March 2008, p. 185.

◀◀◀ BIBLIOGRAPHY

2002 Consumer Profile, Recording Industry Association of America (RIAA), Washington, DC.

Abraham, Jay, 2000, Getting Everything You Can Out of All You've Got, Piatkus Publishers, London.

Anderson, Chris, 2008, The Long Tail: Why the Future of Business is Selling Less of More, Hyperion, Chicago.

Beato, Greg, 2005, 'Twenty-Five Years of Post-it Notes', from The Rake, April 2005, viewed 9 October 2009 <http://www.therake.com/reporting/features/twenty-five-years-post-it-notes>

Benammar, Karim, 1999, Abundance and scarcity: concepts and rhetoric in ecology, economics, and eco-ethics, Acta Institutionis Philosophiae et Aestheticae (17).

Bennett-Goleman, Tara, 2001, Emotional Alchemy: How the Mind Can Heal the Heart, Random House, New York.

Bickerdyke, I, Lattimore R and Madge, A, 2000, Business Failure and Change: An Australian Perspective, Productivity Commission Staff Research Paper, AusInfo, Canberra.

Bilstein, Frank F, Luby, Frank and Simon, Hermann, 2006, Manage for Profit, Not for Market Share: A Guide to Greater Profits in Highly Contested Markets, HBS Press, viewed 9 October 2008 <http://hbswk.hbs.edu/archive/6314.html>

Brodkin, John, 2008, 'IDC report: Data creation outstrips storage for first time', Computerworld, viewed 14 July 2008 <http://www.computerworld.com.au/index.php/id;1049337788>

Bronson, Po, 1999, 'What's the Big Idea?', Stanford Magazine online, viewed 8 July 2008 <http://www.stanfordalumni.org/news/magazine/1999/sepoct/articles/bhatia.html>

Brynjolfsson, Erik, Hu, Yu Jeffrey and Simester, Duncan, 2007, Goodbye Pareto Principle, Hello Long Tail: The Effect of Search Costs on the Concentration of Product Sales.

BT Technology Timeline, viewed 9 October 2008 <www.btplc.com/innovation/news/timeline/index.htm>

Burton, D, Weinberg, R and Yukelson, D, 1998, The goal effectiveness paradox in sport: examining the goal practices of collegiate athletes, The Sport Psychologist, 12(4).

Canfield, Jack, Hansen, Mark Victor & Hansen, Patty, 1996, Condensed Chicken Soup for the Soul, Health Communications Inc, Florida.

Carney, Brian, 2003, 'Price Cuts Can't Save the Music Business', Wall Street Journal Europe, 22 September, 2003.

Clarke, Arthur C [et al.], 1977, preface by John D. deButts, introduction by Thomas E. Bolger, The Telephone's First Century - And Beyond : Essays on the Occasion of the 100th anniversary of Telephone Communication, Thomas Y. Crowell, New York.

Clifford, Donald K Jr. and Cavanaugh, Richard E, 1988, The Winning Performance: How America's high-growth midsize companies succeed, Bantam Books, London.

BIBLIOGRAPHY ▶ ▶ ▶

Covey, Stephen, 1989, The Seven Habits of Highly Effective People, Simon & Schuster, New York.

Davidson, Richard J and Lutz, Antoine, 2008, 'Buddha's Brain: Neuroplasticity and Meditation', IEEE Signal Processing Magazine, January 2008.

de Bono, Edward, 1992, Sur/Petition: Creating Value Monopolies When Everyone Else is Merely Competing, HarperBusiness, New York.

Dove, Rita, 1993, 'To Make a Prairie', The Key Reporter, Fall 1993.

Drucker, Peter, 1966, The Effective Executive, Harper and Row, New York.

Drucker, Peter, 1985, Innovation and Entrepreneurship: Practice and Principles, Harper & Row, New York.

Farnadale, Nigel, 2008, 'Tim Berners-Lee: a very British boffin', Telegraph.co.uk, 30 March 2008, viewed 9 October 2008 <http://www.telegraph.co.uk/connected/main.jhtml?xml=/connected/2008/03/30/sv_timbernerslee.xml&page=3>

Ferriss, Timothy, 2007, The 4-Hour Work Week, Random House, New York.

Gerber, Michael E, 1995, The E-Myth Revisited: Why Most Small Businesses Don't Work and What to Do About Them, HarperCollins, New York.

Gladwell, Malcolm, 2000, The Tipping Point: How Little Things Can Make a Big Difference, Little Brown, New York.

Goleman, Daniel, 1996, Emotional Intelligence, Bloomsbury Publishing, London.

Griffin, Michelle, The Big Squeeze, The Age, viewed 10 October 2008 <http://www.theage.com.au/articles/2004/01/31/1075340890745.html>

Hansen, Katharine, 2000, Foot in the Door: Networking Your Way Into the Hidden Job Market, Ten Speed Press, California.

Hansen, Mark Victor and Allen, Robert G, 2005, Cracking the Millionaire Code: Your Key to Enlightened Wealth, Random House, Sydney.

'Harry Potter and Me', BBC Christmas Special, 13 November 2002, transcription viewed 10 October 2008 < http://www.accio-quote.org/articles/2001/1201-bbc-hpandme.htm>

'Hollywood's Master Storyteller', CNN.com, viewed 7 July 2008 <http://www.cnn.com/CNN/Programs/people/shows/spielberg/profile.html>

Janda, Michael, 21 May 2008, 'Net starts to overtake TV', ABC Online, viewed 14 July 2008 <http://www.abc.net.au/news/stories/2008/05/21/2251210.htm>

Janov, Arthur, 2006, Primal Healing: Access the Incredible Power of Feelings to Improve Your Health, New Page Books, New Jersey.

◀◀◀ BIBLIOGRAPHY

Jordan, Michael and Hatfield, Tinker, 2006, Driven from Within, Simon & Schuster, Sydney.

Kaplan, Leslie S, 1993, Coping With Peer Pressure, The Rosen Publishing Group, New York.

Lacoste, Elisabeth Autore and Chalmin, Philippe, 2007, From Waste to Resource: 2006 World Waste Survey, Rilegatura Paperback, Italy.

Leake, Jonathan, 25 March 2007, '60 years on, IQ test tells us how we age', Times Online, viewed 14 July 2008 <http://www.timesonline.co.uk/tol/news/uk/science/article1563915.ece>

LeDoux, Joseph E, 1996, The emotional brain: The mysterious underpinnings of emotional life, Simon & Schuster, New York.

Lerner, B S, Ostrow A C, Yura M T and Etzel E F, 1995, The effects of goal setting and imagery training programs on the free-throw performance of female basketball players, The Sport Psychologist (10).

Leskovec, Jure and Horvitz, Eric, 2007, Planetary-Scale Views on an Instant-Messaging Network, Microsoft Research Technical Report.

Levenstein, Steve, 2008, 'Nose Celebrity' Tissues for High Sneezers, InventorSpot, viewed 10 October 2008 <http://inventorspot.com/articles/nose_celebrity_tissues_high_stat_10272>

Loer, Stephanie, 1999, 'All about Harry Potter from Quidditch to the future of the Sorting Hat', Boston Globe, 18 October 1999.

Mandela, Nelson, 1994, Long Walk to Freedom: The Autobiography of Nelson Mandela, Little, Brown and Company, Sydney.

Maslow, Abraham, 1943, A Theory of Human Motivation, Psychological Review (50).
McDonald's website, viewed 6 June 2008 <http://www.mcdonalds.com/corp/news/fnpr/2008/fpr_012808.html>

Memorable quotes from Field of Dreams, The Internet Movie Database, viewed 9 October 2008 <http://imdb.com/title/tt0097351/quotes>

Memorable quotes from Six Degrees of Separation, Internet Movie Database, viewed 14 July 2008 <http://www.imdb.com/title/tt0108149/quotes>

Milgram, Stanley, 1967, The small-world problem, Psychology Today (1).

Moss Kanter, Rosabeth, 2001, Evolve!: Succeeding in the Digital Culture of Tomorrow, Harvard Business Press.

Nardi, Bonnie, Whittaker, Steve and Schwarz, Heinrich, 2000, It's Not What You Know, It's Who You Know: Work in the Information Age, First Monday peer-reviewed journal on the Internet, (5)5, viewed 14 July 2008, <http://www.firstmonday.org/Issues/issue5_5/nardi/>

Nietzsche, Friedrich, 1974 (1882), The Gay Science: With a Prelude in Rhymes and an Appendix of Songs, translated, with commentary, by Walter Kaufmann, Vintage Books, New York.

BIBLIOGRAPHY ▶▶▶

Peters, Tom, 1994, The Tom Peters Seminar: Crazy Times Call for Crazy Organizations, Vintage Books, New York.

Ruthven, Phil, 'You never had it so good', Qantas Magazine, March 2008.

Ryan, Oliver, 2007, 'How to succeed in business: Meditate', Fortune, 20 July 2007.

Schulz, Don E, Tannenbaum, Stanley I and Lauterbon, Robert F, 1994, The New Marketing Paradigm, NTC Business Books, Chicago.

Seligman, Martin E PhD, 1998, Learned Optimism: How to Change your Life and Mind, Free Press, New York.

Smith, Ethan, 2004, 'Music Industry Sounds Upbeat as Losses Slow', Wall Street Journal, January 2, 2004.

Snarey, J R and Vaillant, G E, 1985, How lower- and working-class youth become middleclass adults: The association between ego defense mechanisms and upward social mobility, Child Development, 56(4).

Stålenheim, P, Perdomo, C and Sköns, E, 'Military expenditure', SIPRI Yearbook 2008, Oxford University Press, Oxford.

Stanley, Thomas J. and Danko, William D, 1996, The Millionaire Next Door: the Surprising Secrets of America's Wealthy, HarperCollins Publishers, Sydney.

Syder, C Richard (ed), 2000, Handbook of Hope: Theory, Measures, and Applications, Elsevier Science & Technology Books, Chicago.

The Body Shop website, viewed 14 July 2008 <http://www.thebodyshop.com/bodyshop/values/support_community_trade.jsp>

The World's Billionaires 2008, Forbes.com, viewed 8 July 2008 <http://www.forbes.com/business/billionaires/>

Thomas, G Scott, 2008, 'Where America's most stressful places are', Bizjournal, 11 February 2008, viewed 10 October 2008 <http://www.bizjournals.com/edit_special/62.html>

Thoreau, Henry David, 1980 (1854), Walden, Penguin Books, Sydney.

TomPeters! blog, viewed 14 July 2008 <http://www.tompeters.com/entries.php?note=009440.php>

Trump, Donald and Schwartz, Tony, 1987, Trump/The Art of the Deal, Random House, New York.

Trump, Donald, 2004, The Way to the Top, Crown Business, New York.
Weinberg, R, Burton, D, Yukelson, D and Weigand, D, 2000, Perceived goal setting practices of Olympic athletes: an exploratory investigation, The Sport Psychologist, 14(3).

Welch, Jack & Suzy, 2005, Winning, New York, HarperCollins Publishers.

Wetmore, Donald, 2000, 'Time's a Wastin', Training and Development Magazine.

◀◀◀ BIBLIOGRAPHY

Wiedeking's Strategy for Porsche: Image Builds Business', 2002, Automotive News, November 18, 2002.

Wikipedia, Donald Trump, viewed 14 July 2008 <http://en.wikipedia.org/wiki/Donald_Trump>

Wikipedia, Eamonn Coghlan, viewed 14 July 2008 <http://en.wikipedia.org/wiki/Eamonn_Coghlan>

Wikipedia, Moore's Law, viewed 14 July 2008 <http://en.wikipedia.org/wiki/Moore's_law>

Wikipedia, Parkinson's Law, viewed 10 October 2008 <http://en.wikipedia.org/wiki/Parkinson's_law>

Wikipedia, Rubik's Cube, viewed 9 October 2008 <http://en.wikipedia.org/wiki/Rubik's_Cube>

Wikipedia, Yuichiro Miura, viewed 14 July 2008 <http://en.wikipedia.org/wiki/Yuichiro_Miura>

World Institute for Development Economics Research of the United Nations University, World Income Inequality Database V2.0c May 2008, viewed 20 June 2008 <http://www.wider.unu.edu/research/Database/en_GB/database/>

Powerful and insightful...

In the last couple of years, we have completed 3 workshops with a similar theme and one of those was a 7-day program in the USA with a high profile speaker who is considered to be America's leading success coach (won't mention names but he is well known internationally).

The two and a half days with Paul was far more powerful and insightful than any other program we have attended. We left with:

- *new awareness of sub conscious blockages*
- *clarity on how to make goal setting simple and fun (rather than overwhelming)*
- *inspiration, encouragement and motivation to push through our blocks and achieve success in our lives*
- *renewed respect and love for each other*
- *stronger understanding of the power of the mind.*

In an era where we are bombarded with educational workshops that somehow always seem to come across as another means of wealth creation for the speakers, it was an absolute delight to be on the receiving end of your genuine desire to help and guide others towards achieving a breakthrough to success.

Michelle and John McCarthy

No BS...

The fact that you don't waffle on with 'I'm a guru - I know everything' type bullshit (that a lot of other people in your industry do) is pretty special. It's obvious to me that you know a great deal about what you teach, but what I personally found inspiring is that you came across as an un-pretentious, down-to-earth Aussie bloke who is happy to tell it how it is!

Nick Cownie

Putting together the pieces of the puzzle…

The Mental Toolbox workshop was truly a life-changing event for me. I have explored many aspects of personal development over the years and have always taken something good from each source, but before your workshop I always felt that I was taking a jigsaw puzzle approach to changing my life. I'd take this bit from Tony Robbins, something else from Deepak Chopra and so on. But your Mental Toolbox has put all the pieces together for me in a most practical way. That's what makes your stuff so irresistible - you take the most spiritual and life-changing things and put them into such an easy-to-follow, practical program - one can't help but follow it. The challenges of running my own business and balancing other aspects of life are a lot easier now.

Steve Quartermaine

Powerful tool!

To know that I can choose to take positive steps to achieve my dreams is very empowering. The Mental Toolbox workshop has been a really positive experience for me. Thank you so much.

Penny Pippos

I never looked back…

Before I met you, Paul, I had seen quite a few counsellors, psychologists and psychiatrists and they all seemed to make me feel like life was very hard and they gave me silly labels like 'major depressive syndrome'. Then one day I had an hour with you and I have never looked back. I went from being a very depressed teenager who experienced panic attacks to a confident young woman. I've travelled the world, have a great career, a wonderful partner and loads of friends. Life couldn't be more perfect… It's been 9 years since I saw you and I haven't seen or felt the need to see any type of counsellor in that time. I still remember what you taught me.

Rachelle Zieglar

PAUL BLACKBURN

Paul Blackburn has taught more than 400,000 people how to better their lives during his three decades as a success coach, counsellor, author, instructor and keynote speaker.

Paul is the founder and chief instructor of Quantum Orange, a training organisation that helps people to reach their personal and professional potential.

Paul's client list includes chief executives in ASX 200 companies, and his top 10 clients are worth more than $200m between them.

Paul's down-to-earth style has been favoured by Olympic athletes, sales teams, educators and Australian Government departments, as well as the people who lost their homes in the 2003 Canberra bushfires.

Dozens of Paul's clients acknowledge him as the single most influential factor in their 'millionaire status', while hundreds more claim that the practices and concepts taught to them by Paul helped them to overcome terminal illness, infertility or depression. Paul's techniques also helped him recover from an aggressive cancer in 2003.

An inspiring speaker, Paul's audience size ranges up to six thousand, and his presentations are marked by their relevance, value and contagious energy. As one of his students noted, "It is not possible to listen to Paul and resist change. Paul has the ability to inspire even the most negative person to change their life for the better."

Paul is also a successful author. After more than ten years in print, Paul's first book, Beyond Success, remains a best seller.

Paul has built Australia's premier coaching business, all the while maintaining a strong marriage and a loving family life. Paul and his wife of 33 years, Mary, have two adult children and live on a property outside Canberra, Australia.

www.ingramcontent.com/pod-product-compliance
Lightning Source LLC
Chambersburg PA
CBHW070250010526
44107CB00056B/2413